Poetry Slam

Poetry Slam

The
Competitive Art
of
Performance Poetry

edited by
Gary Mex Glazner

Manic D Press
San Francisco

A special thanks to Marc Smith, Stephanie Samualson, Margaret Victor, Bob Holman, Juliette Torrez, Danny Solis, Michael Brown, Erkki Lappalainen, Micheal Scofield, George Whitman, Patricia Smith, Dean Hacker, Cin Salach, Mark Messing, Sheila Donohue, David Kodesky, Jennifer Joseph, and all the many people who helped make this project possible.

The publication of this book is supported by a grant from the California Arts Council.

Cover design: Tracy Cox

Library of Congress Cataloging-in-Publication Data

Poetry slam : the competitive art of performance poetry / edited by Gary Glazner.
    p. cm.
 ISBN 0-916397-66-1 (pbk. : alk. paper)
 1. American poetry--20th century. 2. Oral interpretation of poetry--Competitions. 3. Performing arts--Competitions. 4. Poetry--Competitions. 5. Poetry--Authorship. I. Glazner, Gary, 1957- II. Title.
 PS615 .P629 2000
  811'.5408--dc21

                                 00-009545

Contents

A poem is the very image of life expressed in its eternal truth.

— Percy Bysshe Shelley

Poetry Slam: An Introduction
Gary Mex Glazner

"The points are not the point, the point is poetry."
— Allan Wolf

A poetry slam is a performance contest: judges are chosen from the audience and asked to rate each performer's poem from one to ten. Every poet is given three minutes to read an original poem. For three minutes, these poets own the stage, they take the room. They step up to the microphone and let fly.

In 1986, Marc Smith started the Poetry Slam in Chicago with the idea of giving the audience a voice, letting the audience say if they liked a poem. By cultivating their participation, poetry slams build an audience for poetry, bringing everyday workers, bus drivers, waitresses, and cops to a poetry reading and letting them cut loose.

Holding poetry competitions is not a new idea. The Greeks gave laurel crowns to the winning poets in the ancient Olympics. Basho made his living traveling the Japanese countryside judging haiku contests. From Africa we get "signifying," word battles. Cervantes' classic *Don Quixote*, book II chapter XVI, published in 1615, contains this gem, "just now his thoughts are absorbed in making a gloss on four lines that have been sent him from Salamanca, which I suspect are from some poetical tournament," and this footnote: "Justas Literarias: literary or poetical jousts or tournaments, in which the compositions of the competitors were recited in public, and prizes awarded by appointed judges, were still frequent in the time of Cervantes.[1]" In the '60s, Anne Waldman and Ted Berrigan donned boxing shorts and sparred poetic in New York. Al Simmons, a disciple of Berrigan, started holding poetry bouts in Chicago in the '80s. These bouts moved to New Mexico and became the Taos Heavyweight Poetry Championship.

Shifting the city where the National Poetry Slam is held each year and more importantly giving each city ownership of the slam has led to tremendous growth. The first National Poetry Slam which I produced in San Francisco in 1990 with teams from Chicago, New York, and San Francisco has exploded to more than

50 cities represented recently in Chicago for the Slam's tenth anniversary. In addition to the growth in the United States, the slam has gone global with championships taking place in England, Germany, Israel, and Sweden.

Allen Ginsberg, referring to the Poetry slam, said, "...It cultivates the field of poetry in every direction and is a healthy mental sport.[2]"

Lorca once said, "Theater is poetry that rises from the book and becomes human enough to talk and shout, weep and despair.[3]"

This is the spirit of Slam poetry.

[1]*Don Quixote*, Book II Chapter XVI, pg. 608. Miguel de Cervantes. Random House: New York, 1949.
[2]Interview with Allen Ginsberg, CBS News, New York, 1/29/97.
[3]Federico Garcia Lorca, *Selected Poems*, edited by Christopher Maurer. Penguin Books: New York 1997, pg. xv., originally from *Obras completas*, II: 673, Arturo del Hoyo, ed 3 vols. Madrid: Aguilar, 1986.

S L A M

The Rules

Shocking to have rules for poetry. Perhaps not so strange if you consider poetic form. The 14 lines and rhyme scheme of the sonnet. The season word and syllable count of the haiku. The repeats in the pantoum. In the simplest sense, the rules of the National Slam give the poems a form in which to be presented. I make the distinction of National Slam versus local slam, because on the local level anything goes. You may decide how you want to run your slam and are encouraged to experiment and find what works for your audience. For instance some Slams use live bands or DJs to accompany the poets. Others play with costuming and props, giving a more theatrical flair.

A participant in the annual National Poetry Slam enters a world unlike any other poetry reading. At the Nationals the rule book is thick and convoluted, the result of years of efforts to make the competition as fair as possible. Since the judges are giving an arbitrary number to your life's work, the slam can break your heart if you care too much about the rules and the scores, unless, of course, you win. As a rule, the winners have no complaints about the rules. The main regulations at the National Poetry Slam in an extremely simplified version are as follows:

The Three Minute Rule

The poem must be read in 3 minutes or less. There is a time penalty deduction of .5 point for every ten seconds you go overtime. You will notice as you read the poems in this book that all of them may be read in under three minutes. There is one poet who has lost two National Poetry Slam titles by going over time. He now wears a stopwatch around his neck.

The No Prop or Costumes Rule

No props or costumes may be used. This has led to wild discussions about whether outrageous clothing is considered a costume. Even more dramatic was the battle over whether to consider a certain poet's naked chest a prop.

POETRY

Who Wrote the Poem Rule

Each poet must have written the poem he or she performs. Each poet performs only once in each round. Pretty simple until you add in group pieces. This has led to many late night discussions regarding the authorship of poems.

Scoring Poems

At the Nationals, five judges each score the poems from zero to 10, with 10 being the highest score. After each poem, the judges hold up Olympic-style score cards, the highest and lowest scores are thrown out, and the other three scores are added up, with 30 being the highest possible score for each poem. The judges are encouraged to use decimal points to help avoid a tie. Some local Slams have a wider range of scores, with negative infinity being the lowest score. The judges are asked to rate the poems on the performance and the writing, adding up the values and giving a single score. There is a phenomenon in the slam known as score creep, referring to the fact that scores tend to rise as the evening progresses. The unfortunate poet randomly selected to go first rarely has a chance to win. Score Creep also refers to a poet who is inordinately enamored of the competition and drones on endlessly reciting every win and loss complete with scores to the decimal point.

That covers the basic rules of the National Poetry Slam. For the interested and legal-minded, surf to www.poetryslam.com and request the full set of rules.

The Room
Bob Holman

It begins here. The shape of the room will shape the audience, the mood of the room will give its ambiance.

Whether you're investigating a newly opened boite via brew at bar or reviewing recent acquisitions with the town librarian, you, Potential Slammaster, are sizing up The Room. Could be a church basement — such as the one in Cleveland where d.a. levy got busted for obscenity in 1968, or the Parish Hall where the St. Marks Poetry Project has been holding twice weekly readings since 1966. It might remind you of el Perfecto, the speakeasiest jazz club, Chicago's Green Mill, Mecca for all Slamnation devotees. It could be a brick-walled cafe such as the Nuyorican Poets Cafe, a 501(c)(3) cultural non-profit corporation disguised as a bar in New York City's Loisaida. Slams have been held in subways, at the Apollo in Harlem, in cornfields, poolside in L.A. Every Room, for they are all Rooms, brings its size, vibe, and history. You, O Host To Be or not to be, can assess consciously or un-, but the whole jammy is going to come down to these walls — how can you bust 'em down? And this roof — how can you raise it?

So either The Room is handed to you, in which case the flame is being passed and your mentor can help you fill in all the blanks, or you must persuade someone to let poetry in, which is where this essay begins. There is a third possibility, which is renting/buying a space. If this should be your case, I salute you - book me for a reading (call my agent).

In any case, there will be a Host/MC/Compere/Slammaster in this Room whose job it is to make poetry happen. That is You.

The Job

The job of Host is a just that, job, a service position, maybe a calling, sure. But this is what it means to be a poet at the beginning of the 21st Century: you work, you set up chairs, you're an administrator, you talk with the owner about how the crowd is growing every week or will start soon. Up on stage is one thing, and it should be your thing, or else you will hand that part of the job off. Readying Room, booking poets, publicizing event, planning, conspiring, documenting, dealing with the powers that be at the door (hey! maybe you are the ticket-taker, too!): "The True Administrator is the One Who Sets Up the Chairs," I used to say at St. Marks Poetry Project, where the nightly Stacking of the Chairs is still a communal ritual.

Of course, it is advisable to be a collective when you divvy up the above chores. Maybe you'll be lucky and find these people. But I'm starting off with the idea that you (singular) want to start a slam, and that if you do have co-workers you will impart them with this axiom: The way (Tao of Slam) that you deal with the audience and the owner and the janitor (hey! you are the janitor, too!) and the poets creates the precious ineffable. Because you are about to take the holy art of poetry and thrust it in the spotlight of gladiatorial combat. You will wrap up these opposites so that all within earshot have brains a-dancing. And you'll imbue The Room with Possibility. Poems only ask that they be heard, which is the purpose of slam, and it's in that service that you will create your slam, your show, and hosting style.

Slam Formats

A Poetry Slam is the Olympics of Poetry, a gladiatorial bard bashing. It's different from a poetry reading because of the judges who rate the poems, which leads to all kinds of wild dynamics, audience interactions, redefinitions of creaking text poetics.

If you don't book the poets in advance, you have what's called a Slam Open (as opposed to a Slam Shut). This is the easiest way to organize a slam: place a notebook by the door and have people sign up as they come in. A notebook is good because it quickly becomes a magic record of what went down that night. If you have a time to vacate the premises, you'll need a format to fit that time, a cut-off for the number of readers. There are many formats for slams, but remember: the best slam is the one you invent to fit your particular Room and poets.

The All In: Everybody reads a single poem, then the top two or three scorers slam off for the Big Bucks.

Two Rounds: Everybody reads a poem then, after a break, the order is reversed (or not) and a second round follows. Top scorers again can slam-off if you so desire.

Queen of the Hill: Winning Slammer from one week must

continue on the next week. You can have an All In or Two Rounder Slam Open (as opposed to Slam Shut), with the winner getting to go up against last week's winner for the Big Bucks.

2 outta 3: Four slammers: A vs. B best two of three; C vs. D, best two of three; then winners head-to-head best 2 of 3. Poets get a real work out in this one.

Count down: Poets pair off; high scorers of each pair advance to the next round till only two are left.

The Invitational: Of course you can always invite Slammers, set up grudge matches, draw crowds round their names (partial joke: but if the names are on a flyer, you'll find the poets themselves good messengers spreading the word, drawing the crowd). For Invitationals, the number of rounds depends on the number of poets. If you wish, there can be an attrition system where low scorers are dropped round by round, always to great hoopla and appreciation.

The National Rules vs. the Local Slam

How you run your slam is up to you. The 3-minute Rule is an arbitrary limit set to 1) emulate a pop song and 2) get the Show over in time. The penalties are there to enforce, and it's up to you to decide whether you will or not. Just be fair, remembering that slam is inherently unfair, and know that if you're going to give time penalties for going over 3 minutes, someone has to watch the clock. The same goes for props, costumes, music: rules always bring up gray areas, and it's up to you to decide how important any rules are.

The Show

The greatest thing about slam is its malleability, the way this impossible form (—Quick! What's the potential slam score of Dante's *Inferno*? Answer: -88,721.6 due to Time Penalties—) can do so many things, all of them simultaneously. The slam was invented to fill a time slot in a poetry performance, and you'll probably still want the slam to do the job it does so well: draw a crowd, saturate the audience with power, and set the art of poetry free in a friendly atmosphere. Most Slams are part of an evening's activities, so the question arises, how does the slam fit into a Show? Not just any Show, but your Show; not just any venue, not just any community, but yours. Your job is to create a Show that will attract energy and spirit, that will allow your aesthetic to feel comfortable and active. Here are some elements that work:

Feature/Spotlight/Solo Slot: This is a standard reading, and is generally in the 10-15 minute range. Here's where an ex-Champ can be feted, or a visiting poet can be hired. Please pay poets. Yes, you, Slammaster, generally work for free. How long for the Feature? What time to start? What day of the week? When you start looking at the variables it's a wonder that there are readings at all! You must remember this: anything can work. At the Nuyorican, round midnight (which is 1:30 a.m.) Fridays is the Open Room, which is always an event.

Open Mic: Slam is the lighthouse for the democratization of art, and the Open Mic is where it shines on the world. Anyone who wants to read can sign up in the same book that Slammers signed in on — if they leave their addresses and phone numbers, you can build a mailing list as well have potential Slammers. I'm partial to the One Poet, One Poem dictum but you'll have to feel your way into what's right; another alternative is 5 minutes (Allen Ginsberg when running readings at the Naropa Institute used to give no leeway and would whack his stick at 5 minutes). The community that springs up around the Open Mic always has its own dynamic, and needs tending — if the Open follows the slam, then you can reward poems written during the slam. First-time readers may be introduced as Virgins.

Special Slams: Dead Poets Slams are very popular - I once saw Baudelaire beat Walt Whitman! Heckler Slams, where the poet is nothing but a punching bag for the audience to hurl invectives at, are hard to handle but great at building raucousity. If you have the stomach, then Bad Poem Slams, where the worst score wins, are guaranteed to bring out juvenilia, dumb stuff, and hilarity. Head-to-head Haiku is in a zone of its own — you can find the Rules and Traditions right here in Dan Ferris's essay. Hiphop Slams, Music Slams, Prop Slams, Improv Slams, Music Slams, Group Poem Slams — Slam to get Mumia off Death Row, Slam for Peace.

Late Night Erotica: can function either as a slam or reading. Audience guaranteed.

NB: It's smart to have multiple hosts over the course of an evening. Not only does it make for a livelier event (if a host is a deadener, that you don't need, duh!), build a stronger community, and give you a chance to check up administratively, but you also are training hosts-to-be for the night you've got a reading somewhere else, the only emergency that could possibly keep a Slammaster from her anointed Room.

Press and Other Pre-

Yet another bifurcation is how great slam is at garnering press, but how rarely that press gets a poem in someone's face. Living poetry is still so alien to most people that I still think that any mention of the art is a good thing. I look on journalists as being in a sister art, and since, as Dr. Williams wrote, "It is difficult/to get the news from poems," I like to make it easy/to find poetry in the news by getting press releases and photos in on time, calling reporters, keeping the mailing list and Listservs buzzing, posters, flyers, supporting all the other readings in town. Hey, being a poet is a full-time job!

Day of Slam!!

But let's just say that it's finally The Night! Your first night as a slam host. If you've booked a Feature, you've called the Feature that day with your excitement about the upcoming and dropping in somewhere the reminder that the reading should last 20 minutes (ask the Feature, "Did you time it out? Do you want me to give you a signal?") because the element of Show is the root of why Slams are different from other poetry readings, and you, dear Host, O Slammaster, the Show is yours to shape and form and play as if it were a poem or a piece of music. Hosting the show is creating a work of art.

Meanwhile, back to your conversation with the Feature, you're now saying how it'd be great if they'd get there a half-hour before, and there'll be a ticket waiting (if admission is charged at the door), and "Are you bringing a guest?" and to remind you if you forget about paying them (poets should be paid) because sometimes it gets real hectic up there. If you've booked Slammers, you've called them, too, and informed them of the door policy (it's standard for pre-booked Slammers to get in free plus one), and time limits and rules, so we're all, as they say, on the same page. So now, again!, we're back at the Room on The Night of Your First Slam.

You'll be there early, of course, and will have a pleasant conversation with the owner/manager/bar tender/doorperson — any and all. They are your co-workers, and you'll want to make the slam work for the space. Of course, you've brought your scorecards (the classics are 3x5s plus Magic Markers, but there are some pretty nice ready-mades available).

As the crowd arrives you'll be scouring for Judges. Most Slams pick five judges, and drop the high and low scores. This supposedly helps to keep a single judge from skewing the scores. The upside is that this method wraps the scoring system in Byzantine obtuseness guaranteed to confuse some of the audience (I liked to keep the Method of the Golden Mean a secret; invariably someone from the audience gets heated up enough to shout out that the five scores didn't total 29.7 at all, and then the method is revealed by an audience member in the know, to much head shaking — slam has done it again). The downside of five judges is that it slows the Show — some Slams simply use three judges and add their scores. It's up to you — be creative. At early Individual National Championships there were sometimes ten judges, and still some rounds between Patricia Smith and Lisa Buscani were decided by hundredths! Which is another element, how many decimal points? Judges should be scattered through the house (no peeking!), be various, and obey. Obey means score quickly, and raise scorecards when you call.

When you have judges at the ready, Slammers at the ready, a scorekeeper at the ready, well, I guess you're ready! Let the games begin! Let's get ready to rumble!

How to Host a Slam

Relax and enjoy. Again, there are as many ways to MC this bear as there are yous to do it, so go to it. Remember, you are human, you will make mistakes, but if you are on the audience's side, you cannot lose. If you feel like reading the Official Spiel, do so. If not, write your own. Give props to those who came before, spill libation, pray to the Slam Gods, or tell em all they can take this tradition and shove it, you're a poet with a voice of your own.

Give the judges a big, personal hello thank you! — remember their names! while urging the audience to interact vociferously. Warm em up with some boos. The slam is a mock competition, the emphasis is on mock. Yes, the poetry is serious — listen closely, quote great lines, point out new rhymes. The main goal of slam is to tune up the audience ear.

Explain the rules best you can, deal with score creep if you feel like it. Intro the poets with a Nobel Prize kind of awe, have fun. You want to be fair and pick names out of hat? Do so. Will it take time? Yes. How you spend that time is up to you.

No dead air, keep it moving. As one poet ends, you're on stage calling to the judges through the applause. Amusing patter may occur here, but the idea is once this juggernaut is rolling, keep a move on, get those scores, have a greased lightning scorekeeper (scorekeeper on mic, why not), have another aide writing score on blackboard while you are calling up the next poet. Questions?

Yes? You in the back? Should the Host read one of her own poems? Well, I'm of the opinion no, but that's just an opinion. Id prefer to keep the poets art out of my hosting spiel, or look on that spiel as oral poetry – you're shaking it for the world up there, isn't that enough? Start with a topical Yeats poem instead, or shouts out to Gwen Brooks or Eavan Boland or Etheridge Knight or someone.

The main goal is to tune up the audience ear I don't mind repeating its an oral technique, this explicative paragraph in fact is an oral footnote — it just happens to be written down. Because Slams greatest success is not simply giving poets a new launchpad or getting a crowd engaged in verse bloodletting. When successful, a slam reestablishes in the audience the way of listening that was gradually lost when writing was invented, a process that is repeated in every child as their bedtime stories and poems are silenced when they learn how to read. As Host of Slam, you are First Listener: its your role to listen for everyone, to be the interlocutor between the eyes were used to listening with and the vestigial ears of poetry.

At the end of the night, you'll want to make a big deal out of the winner, mention upcoming events, the Quest for Nationals. Schmooze the press, and, hey, if they're not there, no problem, call/fax/email them in the morning about what they missed. Put the chairs away. Grab the notebook. Be sure to label the tape before you go home. Uplink new stats on web site. Write poem. Dream you're at a slam.

DisClaimer
Bob Holman

We begin each SLAM! with a Disclaimer:

As Dr. Willie used to say,
We are gathered here today
because we are not gathered
somewhere else today, and
we don't know what we're doing
so you do - the Purpose of SLAM!
being to fill your hungry ears
with Nutritious Sound/Meaning Constructs,
Space Shots into Consciousness
known hereafter as Poems, and
not to provide a Last Toehold
for Dying Free Enterprise Fuck 'em
for a Buck'em Capitalism'em. We disdain
competition and its ally war
and are fighting for our lives
and the spinning
of poetry's cocoon of action
in your dailiness. We refuse
to meld the contradictions but
will always walk the razor
for your love. "The best poet
always loses" is no truism of SLAM!
but is something for you
to take home with you like an image
of a giant condor leering over
a salty rock. Yes, we must destroy
ourselves in the constant
reformation that is this very moment,
and propel you to write the poems
as the poets read them, urge you
to rate the judges as they trudge
to their solitary and lonely numbers,
and bid you dance or die between sets.

The Secret Explanation of Where Poems Come From
Allan Wolf

If ever you are in the room with those
Lost in a reverie of poetry,
And struggling to guide their thoughts, they close
Their seeking eyes to help them better see;
If ever you have watched a poet's face
Composing line within a world inside
A world inside some private self-embrace
No other soul can witness nor divide;
Then you are not alone in wond'ring, "Where,
While all their flesh and blood on Earth remains,
Do poets take their thoughts before they bare
Them back transformed? Where is a poem's domain?"
This verse will not reveal from whence it came,
And poets - they write poems to explain.

Teacher
Tyehimba Jess

i want to hit him.

he is standing there and his eyes unblinking.
after the challenge after the setup, here we are nose to nose.
at 7th grade he is tall as me, and i can feel my hand
ripping away and straight through his face even as it lies limp at
my side.

if you were my son. if you were my son. but i know from the
statistics, from the numbers on the sheets that shrink spirits, that
you are most probably no man's son. no man that stayed past the
third trimester, or would it be the third year in which he split? or
is he now festering numbers for a name and buried in the locks
and keys and doors - or maybe under chicago dirt and bullets.

and if he did claim you now, would these same eyes liquefy or
harden or even look through a ghost of a presence in a 12-year-
old life? what would there be left to save? what of fatherhood left

to salvage? what of a man left to give to a boy growing into scars of a man?

punk ass mothafucka. i don't give a fuck what you say, bitch. i shall not be moved. put it in perspective for you. count the drunks on the boulevard. count the bullets fired each night. count the times i am asked for change. count the dealers dollars. count the jail cells. count the lies. now. count the raindrops. count the city sidewalk cracks. count the windows in my building. count the broken glass in my yard. guess what? the numbers are all the same. this is called balance, this is called universe. and all is as it is and words ain't nothin but less than a thang, nigga. words ain't nothin but less than a thang.

give a boy a pen and tell him to write. open his hand past fist to curl into a new life inside letters, phrases, words, sentences stretching into what he has felt, seen heard in his 12 years. have him remember gunshots and mother's curses and slamming, slamming doors inside graveyard prisons. tell him to have more courage than you think you could have because you can't even imagine so many gunshots, so many dead bodies, so many dead friends as he has seen in half your present allotment of years on this earth.

read his stories with the misspelled words, the half sentences, the handwriting scrawled and cramped and twisted into new languages. and when you close your eyes, sometimes you can see his thoughts out loud. his dreams of money, cars and women or even a simple piece of peace he cannot find in the howling graveyard epitaphed Robert Taylor Housing Project.

Backwards Day
Daniel Ferri

Sometimes at school we have a special day
We call it backwards day
Everyone wears their clothes backwards
Or wears colors that clash
I have a modest proposal
Forget your silly backwards hats and tee shirts

S L A M

Forget this stripes and checks together puppypoop
Let's get serious
Let's really shake school up

In math class, for homework
Describe the associative, distributive, and
commutative properties
In dance
Choreograph it, dance it, show your work
Points off for clumsiness

In Social Studies, for homework
Prepare two Civil War marching songs, one North one South
Sing in four part harmony, show your emotion
Points off for flat notes

In English, for homework
Carve a sculpture that expresses Hester Prynne's solitary courage
The cowardice of her lover
The beauty and strangeness of her child

In Science, for homework
Bring in a broken toaster, doorknob, or wind-up toy
Fix it
You get extra credit, for using the leftover parts to make something
new
Points off for reading the directions

On the S.A.T.
Every one of the questions
Will be in haiku

You get two scores
One in whistling, and one in Legos
No calculators

Let's take a stroll down the hall
Let's see who is in the learning disabilities classroom now
Will you look at all those guys with pocket protectors
Sweating, slouching, and acting out

Hey, no one cares that you can divide fractions backwards in
your head buddy
You will stay right here and practice interpretive dance steps till
you get it right

Will you look at all those perfect spellers with bad attitudes
Look at those grammar wizards with rhythm deficit disorder
What good is spelling gonna do you
If you can't carry a tune
Toss a lariat
Or juggle?

You are going to stay right here and do the things that you can't
Over and over, and again, and again
Until you get them right,
Or until you give up
Quit school
And get a job
As a spell checker
At the A & P

My Desk
Debora Marsh

I give you my desk,
the white painted maple,
stately, with clean straight lines, three drawers on each side,
the one my father gave to me.

He carved his initials in the corner, he said, your great grandfather,
his father, punished him because of it.
He made him fill in the grooves with wood putty,
sand down the wood, and refinish the whole piece.
When he was done, he said it looked good,
and that it was a good desk; he used it right through college.
Later, I asked him to do the same, refinish it again,
paint it white to match the 1970s girls bedroom furniture
in the catalog from Sears, so I could put it in my room.

Reluctantly he changed it.
He sanded down the finish, erasing the indentations of the letters
and numbers he had etched over time.
When he placed it in my room, white enameled, fresh, like new,
I cried.
So happy to have that heirloom,
to have my own piece of history,
to have my own piece of my father.
I sat for hours, make-believing I was a college professor,
bank teller, school teacher, the boss.
I did my algebra homework sitting at that desk.
I wrote papers, love letters, and my first poems there.
It has been stripped and painted, broken and glued.

And now, I give it to you.
Older than you by far, it sits in your room
piled high with crayon drawings, coins, trolls, and hot wheels cars.
You're still too young to do algebra homework.
But when you're ready, and you want to use it as a desk,
together, we'll strip the finish,
sand the wood,
rub out my etchings
and paint it to match your bright green and lavender dreams.

Careful What You Ask For
Jack McCarthy

I was just old enough
to be out on the sidewalk by myself,
and every day I would come home crying,
beaten up by the same little girl.

I was Jackie, the firstborn,
the apple of every eye,
gratuitous meanness bewildered me,
and as soon as she'd hit me,
I'd bawl like a baby.

I knew that boys were not supposed to cry,

but they weren't supposed to hit girls either,
and I was shocked when my father said,
"Hit her back."

I thought it sounded like a great idea,
but the only thing I remember
about that girl today
is the look that came over her face
after I did hit her back.

She didn't cry; instead
her eyes got narrow and I thought,
"Jackie, you just made a terrible mistake,"
and she really beat the crap out of me.
It was years before I trusted my father's advice again.

I eventually learned to fight—
enough to protect myself—
from girls—
but the real issue was the crying,
and that hasn't gone away.

Oh, I don't cry any more,
I don't sob, I don't make noise,
I just have hair-trigger tear ducts, and always
at all the wrong things: supermarket openings;
the mayor cutting the ribbon on the bridge.

In movies I despise the easy manipulation
that never even bothers to engage my feelings,
it just comes straight for my eyes,
but there's not a damn thing I can do about it,
and I hate myself for it.

The surreptitious nose blow a discreet
four minutes after the operative scene;
my daughters are on to me, my wife;
they all know exactly when to give me that quick,
sidelong glance. What must they think of me?

S L A M

In real life I don't cry anymore
when things hurt. Never a tear at seventeen
when my mother died, my father.
I never cried for my first marriage.

But today I often cry when things turn out well:
an unexpected act of simple human decency;
new evidence, against all odds,
of how much someone loves me.

I think all this is why I never wanted a son.
I always supposed my son would be like me,
and that when he'd cry it would bring back
every indelible humiliation of my own life,

and in some word or gesture
I'd betray what I was feeling,
and he'd mistake, and think I was ashamed of him.
He'd carry that the rest of his life.

Daughters are easy: you pick them up,
you hug them, you say, "There, there.
Everything is going to be all right."
And for that moment you really believe
that you can make enough of it right

enough. The unskilled labor of love.
And if you cry a little with them for all
the inevitable gratuitous meanness of life,
that crying is not to be ashamed of.

But for years my great fear was the moment
I might have to deal with a crying son.
But I don't have one.
We came close once, between Megan and Kathleen;
the doctors warned us there was something wrong,

and when Joan went into labor they said
the baby would be born dead.
But he wasn't: very briefly,
before he died, I heard him cry.

Joseph Brodsky is Dead
Victor Infante

It moves no snow across the New York streets
this thought, another failed heart
against the storm of brewing snow and hail
that builds across the skyline.
Listen.

We can drink the liberation of
accelerated heartbeats, fist
raised at every small injustice,
as we scratch between the crevices
and underneath the barroom counter
for something, like our freedom was
a misplaced flag gone errant in the laundry,
now lost and easily replaced. Forget

America has a random sort of madness,
its disproportion of needles and cross-fire;
the terror-filled nights we understand,
they speak to us, they have our accent.

We never really lose our accent;
Eliot, reaching for the Church of England,
could not renounce the hard "R" sound
that follows vowels unbidden,
like a stain across his voice,

But this is a Leningrad song
of manacles and straightjackets;
of being tossed amongst the mad
for finding color in the Russian snow.

It is a typewriter tooled with Slavic keys,
that they disassembled piece by piece
till every screw lie separate, as if his voice
would likewise come apart;

Long nights of reassembly, each piece in place

like a well-crafted poem, undeterred
by exile and the roll of Western voices
echoing across the city streets
he did not know. He was forced upon the dream

that Westerners denounce, decry,
pretend is nothing but a fairy tale
taught in schools to stop
the raising of a fist in rage.

We look to drunks and gutter punks to
whisper "we're oppressed," that freedom is impossible,
that freedom's at the bottom of a bottle,
drink it, drink it up,
the only freedom is forgetting,

and all the while we sleep at night
with our familiar demons, sure
that no one comes at night
to steal our pens and
take apart our typewriters;
that terror has a different sound.

Joseph Brodsky is dead. His heartbreak
had a Russian accent, screaming for St. Petersburg
which he would never see again, he died
amidst the New York snow
that turns a different shade of gray against
the ash and sulfur of the air;

But he had shown us there were colors.

¿Por Qué Está Lorca Muerto?
Gary Mex Glazner

As a child they bathed him in
the red milk of the bull.
When he was a calf they
turned his horns to the sky.

As a boy he slept in a bed
of flesh.
The young bull
fed the grain of bones.
He stands in the center of the
ring, waiting for the children
to sing: Today, Today we
drink the red milk of the man.
He comes born to the dance,
never alone.
Horn and steel.
The moment
of forgiveness,
The instant of prayers.
The unbreakable pact.
How sudden the hooves
of the riderless horse.
The curious arrive each day.
Desk empty of poems,
waiting for the pen's return.
On the bed a shadow.
Today you are full of children
can you hear them
from the balcony?
 Can you hear the voices
coming to take you?
Smell the gun powder?
Sweet as assassins eyes.
What will you teach them?
How can they know you?
May we use the moles on your face as a map,
to find the lost lemon of the moon?
How small these trees must have been when you were a child.
Did they shade you as you left forever? Did you ever leave?
The earth holds the molecules of everyone who ever lived, or
    ever will live.
Each breath we take is full of these uncountable lives.
The strum of your poems, the stomp of your deep song.
    Olè, forever olè!

He was the filament Edison forgot.
He burned so bright the glass burst into a question.

¿Por qué Federico?
Would not old age have killed him by now?

¿Por qué está Lorca muerto?
 I speak to you from the cemetery of animals.

¿Por qué está Lorca muerto?
Tan Tan
¿Quién es?
"Soy Lorca,
I hear you are running in circles asking why I am dead.
Why don't you ask me?"
"¿Por qué no me lo preguntas a mi?"

¿Por qué está Lorca muerto?
Lorca: (   )

Now it is your turn.
You must answer.
Take your time.
Take time from
the one-eyed moon,
take time from
ink that is closer to blood.
Seek time
from all the lovers
each moment
they sweat with love.
Place all this
time in the deepest well.
Dip your cup into
the green wet time.
Smell time.
Let it cool
your mouth.
Let time
fill your belly.

Siempre tiempo
You are full with time.
Now is the moment to answer.

The Invention of Jack Kerouac
José Padua

In a bookstore today
I saw a book on UFO abductions
and began to see stars
and strange planets,
vast dark spaces
and bug-eyed humanoids
traveling faster than the speed of light.
I was so moved I slipped the book
into my inside coat pocket.

I picked up a book about
the Hell's Angels and
heard the roar of motorcycles
in my mind, had great visions
of sexy women with beer bellies
who cursed a lot and
ate thick hamburgers.
I went to the cashier
with this book
and paid for.

Perhaps I decided to steal
the UFO book and pay
for the one on the Hell's Angels
because right now
bikers scare me more
than aliens from outer space do.
It's either that or
the influence of the wheel.
If the wheel were never invented
we wouldn't have motorcycles.
And if the wheel had never been turned

over on its side
we wouldn't have flying saucers.
We'd have no truckstops,
no lost time UFO abductions,
no highways,
no Jack Kerouac writing *On The Road*,
just men and women
on horseback
and sailing ships
under a sky filled
with nothing but stars
and the sparks
of roman candles.

Slam and the Academy
Jeffrey McDaniel

"Of course a lot of performance poetry is bad. But I fail to see
how that differentiates it from published poetry."
— A. E. Stallings

When slam first emerged in the national consciousness
courtesy of the media in the early '90s, academic poets vilified it,
saying, "That's not poetry!" Over the years that stance has been
modified to guarded acceptance.

In a flawed analogy, the media compared slammers to the Beat
poets of the '50s. The Beats flourished in a far more conservative
era and were more intellectual, more anti-establishment, whereas
slammers, despite their countercultural poses, are often eager to
be a$$imilated into mainstream culture through MTV,
commercials, movies, even electronic poetry billboards on the
Sunset Strip.

Essentially the slam is an oral art form. One of Slam's greatest
accomplishments is the grassroots infrastructure its adherents have
built geared specifically towards performance, enabling slammers
to tour around North America like punk rock bands, sharing their
words with large, enthusiastic crowds.

A spoken word venue is a literary magazine you can wander

into, where you read with your ears. The MC is the editor. The atmosphere is the typography. And whoever is onstage is the page you're on. You don't need a degree or a letter of recommendation, which is why the slam community is far more multicultural than the academy, which is starving for diversity. As universities nurture talent, so do the best spoken word venues. Go often enough and you will see a person's talent grow. Some venues even offer writing workshops, like the World Stage in Los Angeles and Exoterica in the Bronx.

Until recently, the slam community hasn't constructed much of a literary infrastructure outside of performance venues, leading some people to believe that slam poets don't take themselves seriously as writers. This may tie into the Slam's anti-intellectual, populist approach. Still painfully few presses and literary magazines have evolved out of the slam community. Slammers rarely write in-depth reviews of each other's books or performances. While most slammers are content to print their own low-budget chapbooks at the local copy store, there have been a few notable breakthroughs in published poetry, including Austin slammer Craig Arnold, winner of the 1998 Yale Younger Poets Award. Watching the documentary *SlamNation* recently on TV with the Closed Captioning activated, I realized that this was the first time I'd seen any of these pieces, many of which I know well, in print.

Yet the slam is in touch with the wild, irreverent spirit of poetry, so often missing in university workshops, or stuffy more traditional readings. Like the Beats, the slammers have provided a necessary breath of fresh air. If there's one lesson the academy might learn from the slam, it's that the audience matters. Every poet, regardless of how abstract or esoteric, should have at least one poem he or she can read to a group of strangers on a subway.

The academics initially criticized the slam for its competitive nature, which is strange, considering that one of the main ways page-based poets get a first book published is through fierce manuscript competitions that charge up to twenty bucks to enter, and are often plagued with whispers of nepotism. And arts organizations dispensing highly coveted creative writing grants often have a panel of experts score the applicants, not unlike the way one gets scored in a slam.

Ironically, Marc Smith conceived of the slam as an anti-competition, in that it makes fun of literary mandarins by picking judges randomly from the audience. This puts slammers in a difficult position. They know that the scoring doesn't mean much, but they still want to win. It's like resenting a God you don't believe in. Writing strictly for competition's sake often results in formulaic, predictable pieces, ill-advised re-runs or sequels, in which it seems like the poet is trying to get elected by the judges. Still, even with its shortcomings, most slams are a lot of fun, which is more than can be said about some poetry readings.

An interesting development in recent years is the crossover between the slam and the academy. At the 1997 National Slam in Connecticut, Henry Taylor, author of *The Flying Change* (LSU Press) and winner of the 1985 Pulitzer Prize for Poetry, crossed the aesthetic line and competed as an individual, finishing 75th out of 150. Slammers are choosing to pursue M.F.A. degrees at respected institutions like Cornell, Texas, and Arkansas. Several former slammers are now on Creative Writing faculties: Tracie Morris at Sarah Lawrence, Justin Chin at San Francisco State, and Crystal Williams at Reed. It would be highly paradoxical if slammers were eventually absorbed into academia.

Perhaps, most importantly, is Slam's visible global impact as poets in England, Germany, Sweden, Holland, and Israel embrace it and make it their own. In the early 20th century, artistic movements like surrealism were imported into America. Slam is a cultural export, and that will contribute to its legacy when the literary critics in fifty years look back and try to make sense of what we call the present.

The Adventures of Rufus & Mary Jane, Pt. III: Blues on the Corner/Ghetto Heaven
Ayodele

Rufus footed down
    those Chi-town streets to that
    thwanckety-thwanck bijibownbown beat
    with his brown, polyester bells
    and tight turtleneck to match,
    A Superfly in the buttermilk
    lookin' for a good
        time.

Tripped on a hemp-colored platform shoe
and broke the rhyme.

Mary Jane posed on the corner
      sharp as a Dizzy trumpet lick
      in herbal green threads
      puffin' on a cigarette stick,
                    danglin'.
      High as a kite, about to take flight to
ghetto heaven.

Hey Jack, got some
      time on your hands?
      she asked with static lips.
      Naw baby, my name ain't Jack
      but if you ain't careful
      I might have you on my hands,
      and he stroked her hips.

Sirens screamed like trumpets…

Babywhat'syosign?
      Leo's mine and that
      makes me a lion. But
      I ain't lyin' to you
      when I say
      I dig your figure.
      The fault is in our
      selves not in our
      stars that we are under.

Lingering in the azure above
      where Coltrane blows his sax
      were the wispy white strokes
      of an Abstract Artist
      amidst floating Cadillacs.
      The yellow and green figurines
      on a toy carousel
      in a shop window spun
      around…

SLAM

                    and around...
        and around...
                        and...

Sirens screamed like trumpets...
Baby let's split this joint
        and hit a spot a little less busy.
        And with a finger that beckoned
        like a wispy aromatic curl, that girl
        Mary Jane, lured Rufus
        into the redbricked shadows
        of an abandoned alley.

Slyly, she took Rufus' hand and
        rolled her dry, grassy hair
        in a paper-thin white band and
        pressed her mouth to his
        to a divine golden spark
        lifting him in a dizzy, psychedelic spin—
        a ring of inky disco-avenging angels
        with dark, devilish grins...

Trane was blowin' lovely in the sky...

The yellow and green figurines began to fly...

Afro-angels in Cadillac chariots floated by...

Ru-   fus   was
     fee-   lin'   high...

And then Mary Jane vanished.
        Leaving Rufus, once again alone,
        to search for her in the city,
        while evading those screaming sirens
        and those night-sticked blues
        on the corner.

SNAP!
Sarge Lintecum

Three Stooges in the air;
A dizzy vibe.
Don't say it's me
Just because I can read
Between the smiles.

Look! Just below the ridge line!
Oh Shit! It's at least a platoon!
Papa Dog, Papa Dog, this is Eagle One,
Come in Papa Dog! Over.
Request air strike! Standby for coordinates! Over.

Listen for a siren
On the next commercial.
Make that two commercials,
It's Saturday night.

Beer from a can stinks worse
Spilled on couch and floor,
But the buzz is carefully measured
To complete the circle;
TV, bathroom, refrigerator, and back.

They tell us it's the American dream
So we can look forward to waking up.
But they always keep us making circles;
Go to work, go to the store, buy beer,
Go back home again.

Oh God!
Jackson's hit! MEDIC!
Don't die, Jackson! Don't die!
Don't die, man, they'll fix you back!
MEDIC! MEDIC! Oh God, MEDIC!

Always making circles, tiny little circles,
Making circles, smaller and smaller circles.

Oh, oh, the police are here!
They're mad about me shooting through the wall.
But that wasn't me laughing.

Semper Fi Jewelry Box
Maria McCray

You can have your Army khakis, You can have your Navy blues
but here's another uniform I'll introduce to you.
This uniform is different, the finest ever seen.
The Germans called us "Devil Dogs,"
the name is just Marine, Marine.
We fought the war in Mexico.
We fought at Beleau Woods.
We fought a thousand places that one thought we could.
Our name brings holy terror among the Vietcong,
a war fought bravely, a war some say was wrong.
So *Boys*, here's a little tip I'll pass along to you.
Just get yourself a good Marine.
There's nothing *She* can't do
and when I get to heaven Saint Peter I will tell…
Another Marine reporting Sir, I served my time in hell.

What was it like? People keep asking me.
Is it a voyeuristic thrill you seek for free?
Or is it real concern when I stare 10,000 miles vacantly?

Dead decades duet, plus, I now remember.
A numbed non-response, my only answer.
Never and ever no more the same;
reliving the murdering shame.

Long ago were "Lady Deaths" decades twice.
There were brown brothers I helped Ice.
Delayed stress and Edwin Starr
continue to ask me, "What am I good for."

Ponchos, honchos, afros, corn row wearing chit,
camouflage, c-rations, chevrons, military racist shit.

The poison noise of bloopers, shattering my bones,
killing and re-killing boys with my same skin tones.

Brothers, all in my many hued brothers, long gone dead
and crucifixed shoelaces adorn necks and wrists.
Quonset huts, giving dap, doo wopping, raised black fists.

The gem gleam warmth worms its way under skin.
Too many body bags with brothers going home in.
Too many necks adorned with fingers and ears,
eliminated enemy ears, for favored souvenirs.

Cambodian Red, Acapulco Gold, gone days and nights
bayonet's blade, M-16 insane, one-sided firefights.
Brothers guzzle gasoline, because they took a wrong plunge.
Now, they drink death to kill crabs on throats and tongues.

"Nickel poosey! Yum, yum, Yankee! Hey girl, you Marine too?
Nickel lick, nickel suck, good fuck! For dime me eatum you!"
Normal? Never and ever more no more the same.
Reliving a murdered country's shame.

Dead decades plus, forever I cry. Forever I cry
for those who needlessly died. Forever I cry.

Funeral Like Nixon's
Gayle Danley

Brown and shiny casket
expensive
Draped with the American flag
Poised
resting in the front yard of my girlhood days
Gleaming brilliantly in the honeysuckle April sun

When I die
I want a casket like Richard Nixon's

And when I die

S L A M

I don't want Ms. Flora from the Wheat Street
Baptist Church Missionary Circle #5
to go stuttering thru my eulogy
pantyhose
girdle
shoes from Payless

Let it be known
right here and now
I want the Right Reverend Billy Graham
to lie about me

I want him to tell Channel 5, 11, CNN and World News Tonight
that I Gayle Danley
was the world's most honorable Black woman

Billy please don't tell 'em bout the one night stand
the shot of bourbon
Tell 'em I was pure
a martyr
a goddess (at the very least!)

When I die I want a funeral like Richard Nixon's

As a matter of fact
when I die I want my ass enshrined
right after the 20 gun salute
One (kapow!)
for each one of my sins

Bam bam bam bam bam
for watching Mom and Dad shaking the sheets unnoticed
(I want to be inserted into a marble wall
like a Pope)

Bam bam bam bam bam
for masturbating on the back of the nursery school bus
(I want to be on the cover of *Time*)

Bam bam bam bam bam

for that luscious one night stand
(I want mourners there
oceans of snot dripping from grieving noses)

Bam bam bam bam bam
for playing Doctor with my cousins

I want a funeral like Nixon's
no acne no smell
no fuck-ups
Barbara Bush on the front row

No memory
ass clean
butt wiped

Let me break this down for you:
you see
I just want to die like a white man

blameless
timeless
ageless

Burn, Motherfucka', Burn
Monica Lee Copeland

It's that
OOOh Yeah Ummm' feelin'

Beat burns down the house in flames of lava lamps.
The groping numbness of hypnotized, synchronized souls slightly
    swaying;
Hands hugging hips rounded by biscuits and butter.

Beat burns sweat offa' foreheads.
Couples coupling under the AFRO-Dizzy-Act of sound system
Shoutin' out belts, burps and blurts of smooth noise.
Butties bump!

S L A M

Some fine brother spins his head on the floor,
While a sister spins the rhythm his move grooves to.
No wall flowers clinging in corners of Laura Ashley.
All hands pound out the bass,
As a plethora of Kango boots stomp out in one-two-three's
Deafening, defiant, resilient funkiness.
Agitation mounting into earthquakes of R E V O L U T I O N.
Room becomes rapid pulse;
R I O Tous.
And then there is the
Liquored slur of chanting voices,
"The house, the house, the house is on fire.
We don't need no water.
Let the motherfucka' burn.
Burn, motherfucka', burn.
Burn is the hymn of our decaying nation
Overwhelming the was still of night into
Live ass party
Bababa-Bad!

Beat burns fury into my head.
Cannot shake this noise,
Find quiet,
Make clear, distinct contact
With my soul.
This boogie. . .
Too reminiscent.
Fumbling for exit;
Finding doorsteps sanctuary.
Watching as Detroit dusk drops its drawers on
Abandonment.

Beat burns bewilderment.
For there are homes ablaze today.
Hook-N-Ladders zoom past.
Ruby eyes disseminating over neighborhoods:
Decrepit,
Crumbling,
Hallowed by the smoke of our parents
And their anger.

My skin itches at the words
"We don't need no water . . ."
Looking 'round.
There ain't been no water here.
Rumble of these riots leave us thirsty.
Counting vacant lots
Where once upon homes stood.
And the question:
When all is consumed by fires of
Frustration,
Who must live among the remains;
Dwell within wretchedness
For beating out against
The inequality.

But this beat begins to burn better, hotter, heavier
As some brown hand pulls me
Out of my "What can be done about?"
And into "It don't matter no how, Baby"
Of rousing rhythms that
Unshackle my way down burden,
Caress exasperation,
Purge thought.
And carry me . . .
Carry me. . .
Into a wave of minor chords that yank out the
Pent up,
Pulled down,
To low fo' yo' own good feelin'.
I am among these
Bodies young, riveted;
Firm,
Unrehearsed,
Releasing the words,
"Let the motherfucka' burn.
Burn, motherfucka'
Burn."

Rock'n'Roll Be A Black Woman
Tara Betts

Rock'n'Roll be a Black Woman
Where you thank they got the name from?
Black Magic Woman
Brown Sugar
Copper strings stretched on guitar necks
Tan skins taut on the mouths of drums
Rock'n'Roll be a Black Woman
Plucking as firmly as
Mashing of frets like delicate testicles
jangling under the discord of a well-pedicured foot

Rock'n'Roll be a Black Woman
Eminent as comet tail juice announcing
An ebony-tinged star's exit
Rock'n'Roll be a Black Woman
Furiously embossing the stamp of her man's ass into the mattress
Primacy screaming in breasts that fed you
After tired sweat wriggled between them
She be tainted with funk
Permeatin her like chittlin buckets in kitchen sinks

Rock'n'Roll be a Black Woman
Rock'n'Roll be her blood drippin from
twin tips of a crescent moon
Rock'n'Roll be her kissin Papa Legba at
midnight crossroads
Rock'n'Roll be her standin next to the mountain
that she mashes into pebbles with the edge
of her hand
Rock'n'Roll be her creepin
while you sleepin
through yo veins like Mississippi River mud

Rock'n'Roll be a Black Woman
Workin, jerkin
Grindin, windin
Screamin, dreamin

Moanin, groanin
The sounds on loan and
You wonder where where where
Did some white boy get the name for them blues?
Maybe he was thinkin of some baby-makin hips to abuse 'cuz
Rock'n'Roll be a Black Woman

I Wore A Coin In My Shoe When We Got Married
Sou MacMillan

me and my man:
we are a good kinda dirty room-
      the kind where nothing's in its place
      but you know just where to find it

we are hit and run
      hurricane done been through here when no one was lookin'
        maybe we been robbed!
          kinda messy

but, hell – you could eat offa the floor if you could find it

we's jars of pennies on the bedside
we's saved by pocket change in the sofa cushions
      and a whole lotta makin' do
        a *whole* lotta makin' do –

          makin' breakfast outta cigarettes
           makin' dinner outta dancin' and diet coke
             leave the chicken in the freezer for a party
             PARTY!
             defrost the bird, make a party outta potluck
                 so everyone eats well
         on our first anniversary we will eat wedding cake
we're stickin' dollars in please-forget-me places
      secondhand classifieds sections
      and mama askin' on the phone
        -when you gonna do something with that degree?-

reply
-we're workin'!-
      makin' wings outta words and earthworms
                (and the silk we do spin!)
      makin' wind outta newspaper and colored glass
      & we make us
         get by
we would die on just sheer survival
don't ask me what we gonna do when winter comes
see – snow
    is for sledding
 and green
    is for gardens
      grow hope
      grow strong
      grow black-eyed susans & carrots & rosemary
      grow fat yellow melons
        and joy just seems to follow!
      dance close and hip to hip in the flour for baking
        and the rent just seems to happen!

we's a beautiful round and sloppy kinda gettin' by

this ain't no skinny love-
it's substantial and fat
  (how fat is it?
   this love's so fat that it's qualified to sing the solo in church
   on sunday!)

um!
if i had nickel for every nickel
    i wished tails on and lost
          won
         lost
      wondered over how the hell to clean us up
      oh!
      books and love letters shift beneath our feet
        like autumn falls from trees
         leaves us nekkid
           and nekkid's easy –

you know just what to do with it,
like a song you wrote yourself!
(we make so much nookie,
we gotta save it in jars in the attic!)
oh! –
my degree
degree
de-
gree
pardon me, i digress
into grinning!

can you hear the pennies jinglin'?
the cats scrappin?
3 a.m. tap-dancin'
across the bedsheets
tatta-tat
tatta-tat
tatta-tat tat tat tat

oh oh oh oh –
Oh,
Mama!
PLEASE
stop askin' when we're gonna
make somethin' outta ourselves
see -
we're already makin'
a whole lotta somethin'
outta practically nothin'!

Memorizing A Poem

This is an example of a typical discussion on the Slam Listserv, administered by Tim Woods and Data Wranglers of Dallas, Texas. Sign up by sending an email message to: subscribe-slam@datawranglers.com.

Now it's my turn to ask, because I have forgotten: anyone got any good ideas on how to memorize a poem? I've been working on this one all day, in the bathtub/in the mirror/in my bed/in my car, and I still can't memorize it. I feel like I'm trapped inside Ronald Reagan's brain or something — I can't remember the words to my own poem!   — Eve Stern

Hey sugar — Ask a die-hard stoner girl — If I can memorize, anyone can! 1. Repeat first line, or a piece of the first line, about 10 times. 2. Repeat first sentence, add second sentence. 10+ times. etc. Add in chunks, it's easier. You can remember a sentence, right? and when you get one, you just have to remember the first word of the next line. Sometimes I set up little mnemonics in my head to make the leap if I think I forgot.. O.k., I ended on Remember, so the next one is my dad, 'cause he always told me to never... blahblahblah. Other people I know make sure the first word in the next sentence starts with the same letter as the last word in the sentence before. Also, memorizing while walking or some other repetitive rhythmic movement seems to help me. Hope it helps! good luck on the new one! Here's one of my new lines: "He was the highest light on the roller coaster on the last night of the fair.." — Love, Gabrielle Bouliane

Eve — About memorization... I feel the need to acknowledge, first, a gift (and curse... but then all blessings are mixed) I've been given in this world — my brain loves to memorize. That said: What I do is find the breaks in the poem — either stanza breaks, or just natural breaks where one image or idea leads into the next. So then I've got the piece broken up into nice bite-size pieces, then I read the first chunk, silently a couple of times, then aloud a couple of times... however many times I need until I feel like I've got it in my head, until I can see it. Then I recite it out loud a few times, checking for accuracy if I think I've fucked it up, but otherwise staying away from the page. Then, when it's a solid chunk of poetry — I move on to the next, and memorize it the same way. Then — I go back to the beginning and recite both chunks in a row. If I screw up, I go back to the beginning, only looking at the page if a line is absolutely -gone-. I keep that up until both chunks are solid and connected, then I memorize the next chunk, and then go back to the beginning and recite all three in a row until I've got them down. Kind of like that horrible game that teachers and camp counselors made you play where everyone's bringing something to the picnic, and you have to go around the circle and remember their names and what they brought. And so on. The downside of my method is that you're thoroughly sick of the piece after working it like that, but that's probably true of any memorization process. And the sick-of-itness goes away when you get up on the stage. The good part is that with the poem divided into distinct chunks in your head, your brain can scan ahead to the next chunk while you're performing the first. Also, if you blow a section, it makes it easier to skip ahead without getting totally lost and freezing like a bunny in headlights. hope that's any kind of a help — Kelly McNally

Memorizing - I drive around in the car with the poem on the passenger seat of the car. At red lights I read it to myself. While I am driving I say as much of it as I can - if I forget a line I sit with the empty space and sometimes without even looking at the paper it rises up from some hidden bank of memory. If it does not, at the next red light I look over that section. The first part is data entry into that gray mushy computer into the skull, the next part is trusting that the data entry was done and just letting it happen. I find I like to memorize a poem before I am done editing it, I say it to myself while driving and find all the "trouble spots" where the rhythm is off or the wording is not right and then I edit in my head and make the changes when I get home. I find a freedom in memorizing. I am ready any time any where to give the gift of a poem. — Tamara Nicholl

I'm kind of curious (yellow) myself as to what the easiest road to memorization, or if there is an easy road at all. Do you remember some of your poems word for word or do you sometimes improvise, keeping the gist of the poem in mind but substituting words here and there? In the case of rhyming poetry (of which I am guilty) I guess you have to do the word-for-word thing to keep the rhythm going. But since I've begun writing non-rhyming poetry, I am curious about memorization. And what do you do with your hands? I'm not that gregarious so I'd probably stick them in my pocket (rather than hold that trusty piece of paper). What's the secret? Just standin' on stage shakin' — Ken Green

Even though I don't recite very many of my pieces... I've found that recording myself on one of those mini recorders and then saying it along with the tape works wonders. It's like singing along to your favorite song on the radio. Also when I was in the studio recording recently we had to do like twenty takes, (we would record and then listen to each take) and by the end of the session I had the piece memorized. — Krystal Ashe

Shoot... I've tried all these techniques to memorize. I think I was hoping someone would tell me that if I put the piece of paper up against my forehead, the words on the paper would leak into my brain. The weird thing is: I've never had problems memorizing before; that's always been the easiest part by far. I'm one of those weirdoes who can still remember the phone number my family had when I was a kid, or can recall the address of a house that I visited once, ten years ago. I actually used to look forward to final exams, because I knew that I could remember all the answers (okay, you can stone me to death for this...) I just hate it when my brain is raining on the plains in Spain... okay, so this just means I can't memorize as fast as I used to, and it will take me a week instead of an hour. C'mon, Eve; say "Huzzah! I feel like I have Alzheimer's: embrace that!" In the meantime, if anybody knows how to do that paper-to-the-forehead trick, *by all means* let me know. And thanks for all the support. It helps to know I do have that, which is no small blessing. Gee, Ken: maybe that will be what I write about today, since I have to write my daily poem, no matter what...
— Eve Stern

No, but if you have a copy of the poem in your back pocket while you're on stage, the words will sometimes leak into your brain (through a less direct but nonetheless effective route) if you need them. I've experienced it. It's *creepy*. — Phil West

When I find myself having problems memorizing a piece, I make an audiotape of myself reciting the poem and then ride around listening to it in the car like a new song. That's how I grew up learning the most complex rap lyrics (from De la Soul, KRS-One, L.L.) and, not surprisingly, it works pretty well for poetry, too.
— Peace, Ayodele

Eve, The reason the paper stuck to the forehead doesn't work is because you absorb all the white space, too.... Nobody has yet suggested the device of the classical rhetoricians, which was to imagine every section of the speech (or poem) to be a different room in a house, and you walk into each room in its turn, using the arrangements of things in the room as the parts of that section. But then, that's an idea that has been around a lot longer than typing paper. — Cheers, Michael Brown

Phil's idea for putting the paper in one's back pocket is good for the security factor. We have the poem close. We know "it's there." Additionally, it may be closer to the brains of some of us. — Michael Brown

Kry, I just got hold of a mini cassette recorder for a similar reason. It seems when I'm standing on the corner waiting for a bus (a loooong time to think) or walking down the street, I start thinking out a poem and it's going along pretty good and I'm completing whole poems and I'm like, damn, that ain't half bad. I gotta remember that one when I get a pen and paper in my hand. But of course, when I finally get the chance to sit down and put it on paper I can't remember a damn word and I'm kicking myself trying to piece it back together. So now I'm standing on the corner whispering into a recorder, at least getting the gist of what popped into my head into some semi-permanent form. A few people think I'm one of those pretentious jackasses yakking into a cell phone on the street, others think I'm a flat out nut talking to himself. Actually I got this idea from Gregorio Gomez at Weeds a few years ago, but never got around to it. And now, with your memorization idea, I have another use for it. thanks, Just recordin' — Ken Green

My Dear Sweet Eve, Here's an experiment you might want to try for three full months: 1. add 20 minutes of yoga & 10 minutes of meditation to your daily schedule; 2. sit in the sun for 20 minutes a day, sleep regular hours in a completely dark room, eat sanely, drink lots of water, etc...; 3. ditch any drugs/alcohol you know you can live without; 4. try memorizing immediately following meditation (this is KEY); and 5. if this fails, try memorizing while working w/a hypno-therapist. The first four worked for me; didn't need to try the fifth, though I've heard it works. Alas, alack. — Love, K. Ann Cavanaugh

Hey Eve, Actually I think the idea from Krystal (the mini-cassette recorder thingy) actually might work. Hell, if I can recite all the words to "American Pie" and "Ball of Confusion", I gotta be able to remember my own words when they're "read" back to me, right? Give it a shot and kiss Ronald Reagan-itis goodbye... — Ken Green

I know this isn't going to help those of you struggling to memorize your works, but it might shed some light on the processes of both writing and memorizing. I am lucky in that almost all of my best performance pieces were composed in my head before ever being committed to paper. I would work them over and over in my mind (often while driving the endless L.A. freeways, lots of time to work there) until I thought I had a worthy piece. Then, and only then, would I even bother to write it down. That way, I had the piece memorized right from the start, never had to work on that aspect. Oh, I hear you saying, but what if you had a brilliant idea, but couldn't remember it when it came time to write it down? Well, I just decided, perhaps arbitrarily, perhaps not, that if I couldn't remember it later, it wasn't worth recalling and recording. — G. Murray Thomas

The Fatman
Daniel S. Solis

SEEEEEE THE FAT MAN! FAT ALBERT!
THE FATTEST HUMAN ON EARTH!
walking down the midway with Vicky
to the clank roll and thunder
of the giant ride machinery
hidden behind stretched
once bright now fading canvas
lights lock bars
cheap speakers blaring cheap pop hits
coupons asphalt
and lines for rides like the Himalayan, wild mouse,
black widow, caterpillar, tilt-a-whirl, bubble bounce
presided over by road weathered men
tattooed slack with boredom
cigarettes dangling from indifferent lips

and Vicki says,
"Let's go to the freak show!"

we go to the one where
for a certain number of coupons
you get to view a variety of freaks
more freaks per dollar
what a bargain

I have forgotten most of what I saw
in that shadowy tent that day
there was a black man called Popeye
who could make his eyes bulge way out of their sockets
a couple of listless pygmy goats
and Fat Albert,
not black like the cartoon Fat Albert,
surprisingly not eating,
just sitting watching TV
the barker led the crowd from freak to freak to freak
giving the spiel
and each one did their little freak dance

then it was Albert's turn
the barker talked about how many pounds of bacon
and dozens of eggs and biscuits Fat Albert had for breakfast
then Albert gobbled Twinkies for the crowd
then pushed the play button on a cheap cassette deck
Little Richard tinny howling
"AW Rudy! Tutti Frutti!"
and Albert began to swing his enormous gut from side to side
bulbous fat-filled pendulum pushing open
his shirt's bottom button exposing a fish white triangle of skin
and as the crowd laughed
I looked into the eyes of this man
this Fat Albert
and saw something less than hollow
like negative space
his mind was somewhere else
dreaming of not even god knows what...

S L A M

Slim beautiful women?
a sun-filled road he walked as a child?
Porterhouse rare, salad
and stuffed baked potato?
a *Gilligan's Island* rerun?
the cool hands of his mother on his forehead?
and he caught me looking
and flashed silent anger
"Get out my eyes you sonofabitch!"
and I did
I did

Then Vicki and I
tumbled back out onto the blue skied
autumn streaked midway
and we talked about stealing
that is, "liberating"
the pygmy goats to a hippie farm
but that's another story

and later that night
playing percussion with a reggae funk band
pounding the congas
guzzling Guiness stout
drumming harder than usual
drinking faster than usual
I could not drink or drum
Fat Albert's eyes or the crowd laughter
out of my head
could not shake the thought
that I was a part of a so-called civilization
that lived off
and laughed at
and sucked on
loneliness

and I played so hard my fingers split open
like they hadn't in years
and I wrapped my bloody swollen digits
around a fresh one icy cold

drained it in two pulls on my way
to the dressing room where I burst in
grabbed our drummer David by his jacket
pulled him toward me and said,
"Look, man! If I go crazy and start smashing shit,
and they come and take me away, tell everybody
it wasn't the Guiness, it wasn't the Guiness!
It was the Fat Man!"

America (It's Gotta Be the Cheese)
Eitan Kadosh

Everybody writes about America
And everybody paints America
Because from Jasper Johns to Allen Ginsberg
They are all looking for the same thing
Searching for the real America
The one that lies under the costumes and the war paint
    that lies under the Seinfeld and Springer
    under the bad porn and good basketball

And I am no exception
Except that one night, late last week
I actually found it, this elusive America—in the dairy case at
Andronico's market
Lurking beside the jacks and the cheddars, the goudas, swisses,
stiltons, jarlsbergs, gorgonzolas, whole parmesan, ricottas, and
myriad other imported and domestic cheeses
There—it beckoned suddenly
An immaculately wrapped unbelievably orange package of
American Pasteurized Process Cheese food glory
God bless this country

We pasteurized
We processed
We manipulated this cheese until it suited our purposes
This was engineered cheese
This was the scientific method at work—Jonas Salk Albert
Einstein Copernicus

This was smooth no lumps when melted technology at work—
the lightbulb phonograph model T radio television internet
Nike Air rolled into one
And all for $1.99

I was so moved I broke into the Pledge of Allegiance right there
      and then
I bought Charleton Heston's autobiography
Became a Daughter of the American Revolution

Oh god how I long to be wrapped in golden singles of American
      Cheese
Drizzled with its salty goodness

Oh god put me in a sauna so that the cheese will melt and when
it does it will melt evenly over every square inch of my body
Rivulets of warm cheese will run down my face like tropical rain
caress my body with the lasting wetness of a mouth
Oh god
Take me
Take me and dip me like fondue into your vat of silken
American cheese food products scoop it on to me like a nacho
and let it cool like a second skin oh god cheese food I will use it
for everything

For breakfast melted on an English muffin for lunch in a
sandwich with processed lunch meat processed salad spread on
processed white bread for dinner obliterating my broccoli at bed
on my toothbrush so my breath will be cheesy American fresh in
the morning I will gargle with it and wash my face with a
congealed vat of the stuff I keep on my sink and smear on like
Noxema
I will cook my girlfriend romantic dinners in which every course
will consciously and creatively utilize and emphasize our most
holy of sacraments and when the dinner is over and we hit the
sack I will have a new lubricant —fuck KY!— I'll have a tube of
Velveeta for when the going gets rough
Because it's gotta be the cheese

America land of the free — it's gotta be the cheese

Home of the brave — it's gotta be the cheese
Land of possibility, opportunity and the certain unalienable rights of

manifest destiny — it's gotta be the cheese
who killed Emmitt Till — it's gotta be the cheese
who trained and armed Latin American torture squads — it's
   gotta be the cheese
who shot J.F.K., J.R. Ewing, J.C. Penney — it's gotta be the cheese

internment camps — it's gotta be the cheese
the WWF — it's gotta be the cheese
Kurt Cobain — it's gotta be the cheese
Jerry Lewis — it's gotta be the cheese

The hydrogen bomb the neutron bomb engineered death and
   pantyhose

Mom the flag and apple pie

It's gotta be the cheese

What's Rennet?
Sonia Fehér

   So we're drinking coffee and everyone's talking about TV
shows from when we were kids - *Lost in Space, Good Times,
Underdog* - and I don't know any of them, because WE didn't
have a TV until I was ten and I find myself explaining again
what it was like when I was a kid, just like I explain the names of
my friends: Eliam, Xylon, Huckleberry Krishna and Sylvan
Rahma - his brother.
   And they're looking at me, I'd say you know that look, but
you probably *don't* - the one in which everyone steps closer or
farther away because maybe I'm an ALIEN and the English I'm
speaking has jumbled into a language they just can't understand.
   In times like these, I feel like the ugly duckling following
the wrong crowd and so what that I've been a vegetarian since
birth - because my parents were meditating with a guru and
believed the animals' souls got in the way of reaching the

ethereal plane.

Am I a hippie because my parents were concerned when I got my first tattoo and now I'd never be able to hide from the FBI? Does it make me a hippie that after my first lesbian sleepover, my mom asked why I was so tired and my sister answered for me, in a dimly lit, otherwise sedate restaurant, "She's buttering the other side of the bread, Ma."

I could never understand the fear of coming out considering Mom asked, "Did you like it?" as my stepfather said, "She's taking after you, dear." I guess I'd been prepared for this every time my mom put out condoms for high school parties - to make sure we were having safe sex - or gave me Kama Sutra oils in my stocking at Christmas.

It all made sense to me until I left for college and my friends had been raised with Church on Sundays instead of meditation meetings and mantras.

So my house has bells on the door to keep away evil spirits. So I think this plane is hell and I can only get out by improving my karma. What's wrong with full moons and sacred circles? Maybe we wouldn't need so many sleeping pills if everyone hung a dream catcher above the bed.

Actually, the dream catchers and eagle feather fans really came in handy when the Californians, who admitted they were a little "woo woo" wouldn't buy our house until they knew the spiritual history of the property first. I reminded Mom to tell them about the geometric shape people, the tenants who built sacred geometric shapes in symbolic colors then sat in them and chanted in order to become one with the universe.

Okay. I'm a hippie. But I hate the Grateful Dead. I've never worn patchouli. I shave my legs and my armpits by choice. I drive a Japanese car. I have cable TV. And sometimes, when I really have no choice, I pretend that the cheese I'm eating isn't bound with cow intestines and that my leather jacket grew on a tree.

Disasterology
Jeffrey McDaniel

The Badger is the thirteenth astrological sign.
My sign. The one the other signs evicted: unanimously.

So what? Think I want to read about my future
in the newspaper next to the comics?

My third grade teacher told me I had no future.
I run through the snow and turn around
just to make sure I've got a past.

My life's a chandelier dropped from an airplane.
I graduated first in my class from alibi school.

There ought to be a healthy family cage at the zoo,
or an open field, where I can lose my mother
as many times as I need.

When I get bored, I call the cops, tell them
there's a pervert peeking in my window!
then I slip on a flimsy nightgown, go outside,
press my face against the glass and wait...

This makes me proud to be an American

where drunk drivers ought to wear necklaces
made from the spines of children they've run over.

I remember my face being invented
through a windshield.

All the wounds stitched with horsehair
So the scars galloped across my head.

I remember the hymns cherubs sang
in my bloodstream. The way even my shadow ached
when the chubby infants stopped.

I remember wishing I could be boiled like water
and made pure again. Desire
so real it could be outlined in chalk.

My eyes were the color of palm trees
in a hurricane. I'd wake up

and my id would start the day without me.

Somewhere a junkie fixes the hole in his arm
and a racing car zips around my halo.

A good God is hard to find.

Each morning I look in the mirror
and say *promises me something*
don't do the things I've done.

Sweetspot (or Some Men are Bigger Than Baseball)
Ms. Spelt

Some men are bigger than
Baseball
Cardinals vs. Cubs
bottom of the 1st
McGwire goes to get his bat
his son is on hand to batboy for Dad's
pivotal moment
Big Mac's dad sits in the stands
on his 61st birthday
waiting for his son
to hit a synchronistic 61st historic homerun
of the season
Maris
who hit 61 in 61
is a memory
his kids are in the stands
if you believe in such things
Maris was watching
Hell
Ty Cobb
might have paid it some respect
maybe this will be the one
everyone is pulling for
Sammy Sosa
who once shined shoes

in the Dominican Republic
living in a one bedroom apartment
with three brothers, two sisters, a stepfather
and his mother
who he taps his heart to say hello to after every homerun he
hits his way off the island at 16
barely speaking any English
into the majors at 20
3 years with the White Sox
5 years with the Cubs
streaks that hinted at his potential
then finally started to hit his stride and homer after homer
the year Harry Caray died
and if you believe in such things
Harry was watching
Holy Cow!
as Slammin Sammy
touched
his
heart
leading the Cubs to a long awaited
shot
at a berth in the World Series
Sammy, the one I was pulling for
the one who pulled me back to a passion for
The Game
the only one who could have caught McGwire in
The Chase
in outfield for the Cubs to try and catch this ball
and even he is pulling for him
some men are bigger than baseball
as the pitch spins and hurtles
toward home plate
going over 90
Big Mac leans in
and in a flashbulb moment of camera lenses and mind's eyes
the globe upon which we spin and hurtle through space
stands still to watch this
magic moment of connection
crack of the sweetspot

homerun!
McGwire ties Maris' record!
for eight innings we waited for the record breaker
or for Sammy to close the gap in
The Chase
or at least for the sake
of Cub fans everywhere
hit that grand slam homer
in the bottom of the ninth
that would have sent it into extra innings
but there was to be no
62
no other homers from Sammy
and Cub fans would have to
wait until next game
over my morning tea and croissant
in my regular coffee shop
I heard the unforgettable tone
of
Austin Texas
we sat and talked in an unapologetically rural accent
about things you had to be there for
that we were
missing
the sweetspots
with someone else brings you closer
to that place
to each other
the way a well-oiled mitt
fits the baseball it has been tied around
night after night
since Little League
the only other man to ever fit me so well so fast
is, if you believe in such things
watching
as brisk Pacific breezes blew onto Canadian shores
while the lights of the city
understudied to the moon
pulling me back
to a passion for

who I was with
where we were
what we were saying
that I didn't hear the headlines
screaming about #62
as he walked through my walls I forgot
how I swore I wouldn't miss
#62
sail over the outfield wall
I lean in
to the sweetspot
that moment of perfect connection
when worlds stop spinning and spheres change direction
and find
some men
inspire you
to embrace another's destiny
some men inspire you to embrace yours
some men
are
bigger than
baseball

A Poem about Football
Eirean Bradley

When I pull back and remember
I remember
strength
a palpable hugeness
throbbing in 12-year-old rice paper chests
we were the titans of Michigan Avenue
street ball kings from 2:30 till 5
when mothers would swoosh granite hands
and wave us in frail and battle worn
but now-

it's fourth down
and the bumper of Mr. Sinclair's Volkswagen to go

S L A M

Okay, Lump you bust off the right tackle
and dish it to Greenie
Velcro, you go deep
just watch out for Bundy and it'll all be okay
okay
break

my schoolyard tag
was always
Velcro
sure I was short
and fat
and slow
but I never dropped the ball
on first down I went on the ghetto of all sports plays
I went deep.
on second down you went to the speed of Jay
on third the nimbleness of Greenie
but fourth down
was my domain
my neighborhood
my hands were so magical that I was never picked
last

which for a short fat kid was an
earth
shaking
accomplishment

I could always handle the ball
we were like
blood brothers
the sweat on my palms kissing synthetic leather
like a voodoo binding ritual
I could always handle the ball

Bundy was a completely different issue
altogether
Bundy was 5'5 150 pounds in the 5th grade
a wall of aggression always lumbering in the background

he was built like a refrigerator
with a head
he always had a way of turning two hand touch
into two hand ass-kicking
but he was slow
and if you played chicken
With that newly pubescent freight train
just long enough to smell
the newly acrid odor
coasting off his newly hairy pits
you could throw on the brakes
plant your left foot
and Gale Sayers your way to pay dirt
I could always control that

When he was 16
Bundy got his heart perforated
by a switchblade wielded by another
short fat victim not as willing as I to take a beat down and
Lump went off to Stanford to study law and
Greenie drew in gray smoke slow and deep and
spastically exhaled
gray with pink highlights

I have never seen a diagram
or an illustration of a heart exploding
but you know
when
the chest sinks in
and
the eyes flutter back
and
the arm sledgehammers into the coffee table
and
the cops accompanied by the coroner
will be here soon
and
sorry bro,
but I gotta run
but I promise I'll do a quick Hail Mary

as I leave the doorstep
of your parents'
now childless
house

I never did
seemed pointless

I don't talk to parents anymore

I hate asking
"so Mrs. Greenberg how have you been?"
really meaning
"so how you been since your son died?"
the slumped shoulders
that held all their ever more fragile dreams
in the wilting chrysalis of a boy
when I pull back and remember
I refuse to see corpses
or gravestones that are only good for birthing poppies
instead I see
it's 4th down and
long

long
to go
Okay, Lump you bust off the right tackle and dish it to Greenie
Velcro you go deep
there we are still young
innocent children of god
and my hands are still
magical enough
blessed enough
to lead us sunbathed and bronzed
into the promised land

POETRY

Persona Poem
Patricia Smith

Again. I'd grow tired of it if it wasn't so jolting, so new every time, so sad and blood-washed and tragic. Once again, I stand in front of a classroom of wary high schoolers at 9 a.m. on a weekday morning, and all they want to talk about is death. Purportedly, I am there to teach poetry — I'm armed with earnest resolve, snippets of Gwendolyn Brooks and Langston Hughes and Lucille Clifton and Amiri Baraka, samples of my own work and exercises I hope are engaging enough to overwhelm the pervasive 9 a.m. doldrums. But I'd forgotten where I was, what the pre-eminent buzz was likely to be in this cluttered New Jersey classroom on almost any day: "Somebody got shot last night." "Did you hear, who was it?" "I just heard somebody got jacked." "Hey man, I knew him, he used to go here." "*He dead?*"

They don't want to talk about poetry. They look at me like I'm a fool, having already decided that I am simply a purveyor of dusty hearts and flowers, although I haven't even begun my spiel, haven't knocked them back in their seats with a sample of Mother Brooks' street-soaked blues. They're absolutely sure that I'm clueless — my skin color, easy knowledge of this week's street lingo and my West Side Chi-town rep aren't nearly enough to impress. They've decided to skate through this double-period, passing notes and snickering behind cupped hands. Ten pairs of hard eyes meet mine and say that *their* poetry is brief and violent and final. It can only be read once. Then it's on to life again.

I know that the only way they will find poetry in the events of the previous evening is to enter the story, become an integral part of it, examine every perspective of the tale. I want them to step resolutely into the mind of the man who is now dead. It's a strange, chilling place. And the only way they'll be able to escape is to write their way out. I dump my loosely conceived lesson plan. There's one surefire way to broaden that just-the-facts-please narrow focus of theirs, a way to click those dormant passions into gear. At the risk of sounding haughty, they're never going to look at poetry the same way again. Better yet, they're going to want to write it.

Ladies and gentlemen, it's time to deal with the persona poem. And that would be — what? Let's leave our wary wordsmiths for a moment and turn our attention to coming up with a definition that works: In a persona poem, the writer eliminates the middle man and actually becomes the subject of his or her poem. The voice is both immediate, and immediately engaging. In the best cases, the poem's audience is drawn into a lyrical narrative by someone they want to know better — a taxi driver, Little Richard, an undertaker, a bungee jumper, Richard Speck, the captain of the Andrea Doria. In fact, they become so attuned to the storyteller's energy that it becomes difficult to believe a poet was ever involved at all. The poet, whether on page or stage, is simply a conduit for the story. I happened upon the unsettling world of the persona poem quite honestly, and used it as a crutch for much too long at the beginning of my career as a rhymester. It just seemed natural that the best way to get closer to someone — whether a real flesh-and-blood person or a character in a poem or short story — was to try on their shoes, see the world through their eyes. So whenever I settle upon a subject to write about, the first thing I do is become that subject. I let him tell me who he is — but, more important, I forget who I am. I speak as my subject, not for him. Unless we take a moment to slip on the life of someone we're writing about, we haven't truly written about them — even if the end result isn't a persona poem. Eliminating myself as the middle man was both an exhilarating and frightening prospect. Now that I know how powerful the persona poem can be, I hesitate to share my first attempts at the genre, which stuttered in quite a few ways. It was a giddy undertaking, becoming someone else. The very first persona poem I ever wrote was a playful little ditty called "Single and Hot in the '80s (Or, How I Learned to Love Being a Statistic)." It's in the voice of a party girl who finds herself seduced and bedded down (again) by a guy she wouldn't bless with the time of day if she'd stayed sober. In absolutely no way did I draw on personal experience:

This time, it takes almost two hours.
Reality checks in. The alcohol checks out.
And I find myself making little passion noises
beneath an insurance salesman
who's all Old Spice and flailing limbs...

My chest feels rearranged.
My face smells like sloppy vodka kisses.

And I don't have the heart to tell him
that he's miles away from his intended target...

My first fumbles with persona poems were playful, experimental
and joyous. I was reveling in my discovery of my new throat. I was
a nosy barber keeping up a running Saturday morning commentary,
a young girl learning to jump double-dutch, Medusa answering
her critics, Olive Oyl (Popeye's beau) in a People Magazine
interview, Michael Jackson (finally) explaining himself. I soon
found myself taking on the voices of things that weren't human.
"The Awakening" was written in the voice of a tree on the shoreline
of Chicago's Lake Michigan. But it's hard to work with persona for
very long before realizing its power. Soon the genre became a
survival tactic, a way for me to process the world. It was no longer
simply a way to write, it was a way to think. Planes blowing up in
mid-air. Another young black man gunned down on a city street.
An 8-month-old child tortured and killed by his parents. I was
able to make some sense of the madness by stepping directly into
it. I walked right into whatever had saddened or angered me, tried
on the shoes of everyone there, and when those shoes felt most
uncomfortable, I knew it was time to start writing. Raymond Wood
was that 8-month-old boy. This is an excerpt from the poem
"Creatively Loved":

It took me an hour to die,
my new world blurring,
curled like a comma in my leaving,
lit cigarettes smoldering in my hair.
My legs were bone and paper.
I had not yet learned to walk.
I will reach heaven this way,
a tiny broken circle with one edge on fire.

A few years ago, 466 people—most elderly and infirm—died during
a sweltering Chicago summer:

The sirens outside my window wrapped their wail
around my chest and hugged hard. I coughed, and the sound
startled the air, teased me with a pocket of cool.
I was young again, and the night was loving me, swallowing me

whole—
my sizzling hair, my frozen knees, my shuddering lung.

Twenty-seven people died in Killeen, Texas when George Hennard drove his pickup truck through a crowded restaurant and opened fire before taking his own life. A young black woman was the last person to be pulled alive from the wreckage of the Oklahoma City bombing. A Massachusetts skinhead spews venom during an interview. I met them, became them, in my poems. I heard their hearts beat. I took a terrified peek into their minds. Persona poems are an entry into a world that defies understanding. You don't have to know much about the your adopted persona before you begin to write — in fact, what you're doing is stepping into their shoes while they learn about themselves.

When I began to write the skinhead poem, I wanted to understand a man who unconditionally hated what I was. I knew that we'd begun with the same head, the same heart, looking out on the same world. But somewhere along the line, he went one way and I went another. I wanted to find that space where we began to see separate worlds. I was determined to know him. But that glimpse of his life, those moments of slipping on his voice, trapped me in his hatred. I felt as if I were losing myself. It was a struggle to write my way out. Even now, when I perform the poem, audiences are jolted by his voice coming from the mouth of a black woman. You must always come back to you — the person with pen in hand, giving life to someone — but the more effective the poem, the harder the road back. There's nothing like that first step. Back to the real world.

I ask my sullen students to tell me what they've heard about what happened. Timelines conflict, names and locations change, the details are sketchy. But everyone chimes in at once, because the topic is something that is real and familiar and close to them, and it scares them too. They speculate and dismiss and glorify, testify and deny. They shout one over the other, each one needing to serve up the definitive observation on the violent death of someone they hardly knew. In the end, what we have is: A guy familiar to some of them was found that morning slumped against an alley doorway. There was a bullet in his head. He may have been messing with somebody's woman, robbed for drug money or punished for disrespecting one of the local street kings. He was dead.

I ask the class to take out a sheet of paper. "Write me a stanza in the voice of the dead man." Immediately, there is a howl of protest: "*He's dead.*" I read them Lucille Clifton's conversation between God and Lucifer, Ai's first-person rant in the voice of Latasha Harlins, the New York teenager gunned down by a Korean shopkeeper. The poem begins with Latasha walking into the store, ends after she is long dead. Her thoughts go on. She can think them, she simply can't speak them. "With a persona poem, you can be anyone at any time," I tell them. A few eyes widen, brighten with possibility. Ten minutes later, a buxom student with moon-round eyes and meticulously wrapped penny-red hair offers up this gem in the voice of their community's latest casualty:

So this is what hell is like
I just go on living
In this dead shell.
Got this hole in my head
So I can't hold onto my dreams
Too long

I marvel at her. She blushes, withdraws as she begins to resent being singled out for praise. We talk about how many pairs of shoes there are to try on. The person who found the dead man. His family, waiting at home. The person who shot him. The policemen who show up at the scene. Who's going to wash the blood off the sidewalk? How about his children, who will now grow up without a father? How about children he hasn't had yet? This freaks them out. *What?* I tell him that he was a man probably able to father children, children who will now never be born. There are a few giggles when I say the word "impregnate," but I can tell they're beginning to catch on:

Daddy, why?
Why didn't you think
of how many lives
you were losing?

I take a deep breath. It's all or nothing at all. "OK," I say, "How about the gun? What does a gun think about shooting someone?"

Nobody says anything. Nobody calls me crazy. Just about everybody picks up a pen. Five minutes later, a 15-year-old mumbler, feigning reluctance, picks up his paper and reads in the voice of a 9mm handgun. The first word in his poem is the word "*Boom*." I think I've got 'em.

Superman In the Nursing Home
Rusty Russell

It started with the flying.
I just had to get away.
I thought I was going crazy, hearing things -
voices, sirens, water running behind walls,
and the crying, someone always crying behind closed doors.
It was that super hearing. I had it then.
So some nights I'd fly out of the city
until I couldn't hear them anymore,
way out over the ocean where I could see the earth turning
and the sun rising over the edge of the next day.
Miraculous, made me feel like the only man on earth,
but I wasn't a man. I was a freak.
Then came all those years
of changing clothes in dirty phone booths;
chewing gum on the floor getting stuck in my pants,
cigarette butts, and the smell of winos and urine.
Sometimes the phone would ring while I was in there
and it always gave me the creeps.
Think about it - an anonymous telephone
in the middle of the night on a deserted street
and it's ringing for someone. Anyone.
I never picked it up. I didn't want to hear it -
lives pulled thin over a phone wire,
stories of pockets with holes,
bad breath whistling through bad teeth.
What could I do?
Someone sobbing and sloppy drunk in a bar somewhere
picks up a phone, dials a number at random
and gets Superman
with his pants down in a phone booth.

Believe it or not, this Superman thing started out modestly:
  no cape, no tights.
Just lifting automobiles off trapped motorists,
or catching falling babies before they hit the sidewalk.
But it felt so good, the applause,
the way the Earth girls looked at me,
and it all got out of hand.
I should have stopped after the first bank robbery.
There would never be any cash reward in this
for an indestructible guy like me.
Just "Thanks, Superman,"
and the bankers smiling as I flew away.
All the time they were thinking,
"What a fucking tool," and they were right.
Hell, it was all insured.
If I'd quit then and done something with myself -
forgotten this superhero thing and gotten a realtor's license
or just a full time job with benefits,
maybe I wouldn't be waiting for the TV hour
here in the dayroom of the County Home.
I never saved anyone from this. No one could.

But in a way, it's true, what they say,
that every moment lasts forever,
because I still dream about those first nights
when I was young, before it all started,
flying out of Metropolis in my pajamas
with the moon overhead and the silver ocean below,
and the billboards left behind
like a cry for help I can finally ignore.

Gilligan
Michael Salinger

I am Gilligan
Overturned breakfast bowl sailor cap
Pratfall head hunter bait for your amusement
in livid black and white
A cathode coated clown

Riding on the waves of canned laughter
Lapping onto the lagoon of collective
Consensual
Semi consciousness
I gather coconuts
My sea legs pump the pedals
Of the bicycle
That powers the radio
I sing Hamlet's soliloquy
Accompanied by bamboo geared victrola
I find EVERYTHING
Magician's trunks
Japanese soldiers
Space capsules
And radioactive stuff
I am Gilligan
This is my island
I am your little buddy
I am Gilligan
Prince of tides seated beneath a palm tree
Golden husk perfectly cleaved
By a Newtonian skull shattering free fall
One half lay at my feet
One half flows upstream
Tugboating me along in a dream
And as I sleep beneath the tree
A trained gorilla in a tutu falls in love with me
But I do not leave
Mrs. Howell Mary Ann and Ginger plead
Hurricanes rage I am struck by lightning
Meteors drop into my lap
Yet I remain solid
Resting on one arm
Immovable
Speechless
Clueless
I am Gilligan
Leather facing the facts at the boat show
Rescued from any body of water near the shopping center
Thirty some years a caste away

thirty years
The skipper's dead
Luvy's dead
Mr. Magoo
Dead
And I vaguely recall Maynard
That swinging Dharma hep cat
And even Dobie became president of CBS
At least I'm not selling Bibles on late night TV
Yet
I am Gilligan
Here on Gilligan's Isle

Why Amelia Earhart Wanted To Vanish
Derrick Brown

Amelia asks for forgiveness
looks down at the table like we are playing chess.
The larger pout of her bottom lip is imported from Uruguay:
Ooo-doo-guy.
Her R's and the A's become dizzy ghosts
Distance
The bottom lip, simple as a sentence.
But the upper lip
a complex creature.

Amelia's youth suitcased in the upper lip
- ready for wrinkles.
Lipstuck lipstick lipstock residue in flushed hue
Like she'd been kissing madly
Like she walked off the set of an MGM ending
Cast to kiss sailors ready to die

Her hair looks as if she'd been running with a man
in black and white
through the sets of dangerous cities

Her few wrinkles are just symptoms of sleeping on her face, on
her eyes

she doesn't trust them to stay shut.
Amelia sleeps on her eyes.
Amelia ruins pillowcases with her lipstick

Zip focus into the darkness
where her lips should meet
God,
Those corners.

For now it is dead in here.
The fifth of July.
January 2nd.

The black pockets - empty and full like poverty.
These are not simple.
Endless. Hungry. Surrounded.
Dragging air like jets of the atmosphere
drawing it in
in
in slow motion
drawing it in freehand
into those corner lip pockets.
The separations open and close -
moves elastic in melody with her chest.
1, 2, 3, 4,   1,2,3,4   1
air marches in...
and then nothing more marches out.

I could low crawl inside those corner pockets
grab her gums and see if they're bleeding
to see if she wondered if she said the right thing
To see if there was some sign of wonder or weakness
or nervous.

The way dogs watch you after they've been hit by cars.

A sign that speaks of all normal persons having fear,
a bite in the cheek
a grind in the crowns
something that will give her away...

"C'mon Amelia. Come on. This is not chess, Amelia!"
She says "Shh. Save your yelling for sex and riots."

Peeking at the daylight from the corners of her mouth.
The dryness chaps
I look for bats or
Sailors' initials but
Nothing.

I wait under the quilt of her tongue -
unthawed.
Searching for blood.
Carving letters on her canines...
"Amelia. If you leave, don't you ever come back."

Alone in the cockpit, her propellers began to spin.

Medusa's Diner
Paula Friedrich

Appetizers are easy-
with a flick of the wrist,
seasoned flour and a spoon of olive oil.

On a good day, she lifts her sunglasses,
turning truckers and squirrelly children
into digitally mastered images
she can e-mail to her friends back home.

When her serpents shed their skins,
the papery shells slide down the back of her sundress,
break like potato chips, litter plates of chitlins
and crackle under sandals. Little hands get slapped
for poking them across the floor.

Medusa has the comfort of knowing no one
can look her in the eyes and kill her
at the same time; she misses nothing.

S L A M

Hollywood forgot she was born in the sea,
stumbling on white beaches, snapped eels in two
with an amphibious force, squeezing venom
out of her tear ducts on the days she dreamt of swords,
all mouths breathing "monster,"
every scale on her head tipped the wrong way,
every tongue suggesting different lies
and seagulls only turning into wood.

Medusa's lover is a blind snake-charmer;
His hair stands on end.
When they dance, Medusa rattles
down to her belly and her hips and her feet.
The rhythm is a lover, is a brother is a song buried alive and
moving like
arteries shifting when marble sucks
the surfaces of her feet linen breaking
bread into biscuits for decades to chew on
when she dances, her desire
is a head full of dragons, cunning fusion of flames
blowing up the highway, licking grease into gold
breathing down the necks
of the ones who write bad checks
and adding extra bacon in a bad month.

Her sweat is poison;
and garden snakes on cool mornings
in well-trained flower beds
are the venomous, rollicking nightmare she calls the world.

She can make herself stop,
listen to what is left of the heart,
and still make sure her coffee
hits the gut
like a stone.

My Father's Coat
Marc Smith

I'm wearing my father's coat.
He had died. I didn't like him,
But I wear the coat.

I'm wearing the coat of my father,
Who is dead. I didn't like him,
But I wear the coat just the same.

A younger man, stopping me on the street,
Has asked,
"Where did you get a coat like that?"

I answer that it was my father's,
Who is now gone, passed away.
The younger man shuts up.

It's not that I'm trying now
            to be proud of my father.
I didn't like him.
He was a narrow man.

There was more of everything he should have done,
  More of what he should have tried to understand.

        The coat fit him well.
        It fits me now.
        I didn't love him
        But I wear the coat.

Most of us show off to one another
Fashions of who we are.
Sometimes buttoned to the neck.
Sometimes overpriced.
Sometimes surprising even ourselves
In garments we would have never dreamed of wearing.

        I wear my father's coat.
        And it seems to me

That this is the way that most of us
Make each other's acquaintance—
in coats we have taken
To be our own.

Inventing Jobs
Hal Sirowitz

You're almost thirty, Father said,
& you don't have a job. When people
ask me what you're doing I make up
a job for you. And I have to remember
what I tell them, & not give you
a new job every week or they'll get
suspicious. And if you do find a job,
& people tell me that I said you were working
at one store but they saw you at another I'll be
so happy that you're finally standing on your own
two feet that I won't mind if they think I'm a liar.

Mama's Magic
Glenis Redmond

My Mama is Magic!
Always was and always will be.
There is one phrase that constantly bubbled
from the lips of her five children, "My mama can do it."
We thought mama knew everything.
Believed she did, as if she were born full grown from the
Encyclopedia Britannica.
I could tell you stories.
How she transformed a run down paint peeled shack into a home.
How she heated us with tin tub baths from a kettle on a stove.
Poured it over in there like an elixir.

We were my mama's favorite recipe.
She whipped us up from a big brown bowl,
supported by her big brown arms.

We were homemade children.
Stitched together with homemade love.
We didn't get everything we wanted
but lacked for nothing.

My mama was protection!
Like those quilts her mother used to make.
She tucked us in with patches of cut out history all around us.
We found we could walk anywhere in this world and not feel
alone.

My mama never whispered the shame of poverty in our ears.
She taught us to dance to our own shadows.
Pay no attention to those grand parties on
the other side of the track.
Make your own music she'd say
as she walked, as she cleaned
the sagging floorboards of that place.
You'll get there, You'll get there.
Her broom seemed to say with every wisp.
We looked at the stars in my mama's eyes,
they told us we owned the world.
We walked like kings and queens even on midnight trips
to the outhouse.
We were under her spell. My mama didn't study at no Harvard
or Yale. But the things she knew
you couldn't learn from no book!
Like...
how to make your life sing like sweet potato pie sweetness
out of an open window.
How to make anybody feel at home.
How at just the right moment be silent,
be silent, then with her eyes say, "everything gonna be alright,
child,
everything is gonna be alright."

How she tended to our sickness.
How she raised our spirits.
How she kept flowers living
on our dilapidated porch

in the midst of family chaos.
My mama raised children like it was her business in life.
Put us on her hip and kept moving.
Keeping that house Pine-sol clean.
Yeah, my mama is magic.
Always was and always will be.
Her magic. How to stay steady and sure in this fast pace world.
Now when people look at me
with my head held high.
My back erect and say,
Who does she think she is?
I just keep walking
with the assurance inside.
I am Black Magic.
And I am Jeanette Redmond's child.

Third Letter to Little Brother
Mike Henry

The last time we talked on the phone you were in, of all
places, Los Angeles having left the cherished Oklahoma
homeland in the beginnings of a long, circuitous journey
scripted in the scattered bones of a year past and tonight I
remember it all. Our years together with red wine and road trips
when love grew like the tall green in your basement and I
remember the bust, and the trial, and the time with you away
and I remember when you told me you had applied for a
teaching job in China. Holy shit, China! But the pay is great,
you said, I gotta make some money to pay for the lawyer and the
fine, you said. I won't spend that much money 'cause I can't
speak Chinese that well, you said. It's only a year, you said.
"Only a year," and the words echo like a coffee shop headache
against my bones, remembering the one who left, wondering
who'll come home.

So I read on in this letter that you wrote me and you tell me
about your new Chinese apartment where nothing matches that
has a water container in the fridge shaped like a cow's stomach
that you want to bring home with you just to annoy a future wife
with, "but honey… it's priceless." You tell me you taught your

first class the other day, had to give English nicknames to all
your students. The girls' names were taken from the names of all
of your ex-girlfriends. Good planning on your part to have had
so many. The boys' names were taken from the Monkees, Sex
Pistols, Beatles, Grateful Dead, Peter, Greg, and Bobby from the
Brady Bunch.

The paper reads my eyes, wondering if you miss anything
yet. Scribbled words sing songs of supermarkets laying prone,
vulnerable to 4:00 a.m. drunkard cravings. Of playing "The
20,000 Dollar Pyramid" two chairs facing, one back to the
television with the sound turned off. Of petrochemical chariots
erasing the road behind them given cheap beer and glory for the
morning on a gas card. Of Denny's "Big Slam" breakfast. Of
dosing our friend Chad, who had never tried acid, by throwing
pieces of microwave popcorn for him to catch in his mouth, one
with the blotter folded inside. Finally, of Leo's Bar-B-Q, south
side Oklahoma City shoulda been Texas dripping blues and
carnage with a fat pink swine dancing on the sign like a pool
hall painting of Miss Piggy's naked honeymoon, hey wait a
minute. These are the same things that I miss.

There's a quote from somebody somewhere that says "gone
are the days where we stopped to decide where we should go.
Now we just run." Yeah, sometimes farther than the mightiest of
gas cards, the most undiscovered public highway. I'll count a
year in the Texas night, in the fading of leather hanging on my
closet door, in the things we miss together.

Grandfather's Breath
Ray McNiece

"You work. You work, Buddy. You work."
Word of immigrant get-ahead grind I hear
huffing through me, Grandfather's breath
when he's come in from Saturday's keep-busy chores,
fending up a callused hand to stop
me from helping him, haggard cheeks puffing
out like work clothes hung between tenements,
doubled-over under thirty-five years a machine
repairman at the ball bearing factory,

especially torpedoes. He busted butt
for the war effort, for profiteers, for overtime pay
down payment on a little box of his own,
himself a refugee of the European economy
washed ashore after the "war to end all wars,"
cheap labor for the winners.

I hear his youth prodding through the hayfields
above Srednevas, and the train that wheezed
and lumbered to the boat where he heave-hoed
consumptive sisters one, two, overboard.
I hear him scuffling along the factory-smoke choked
streets of Cleveland, coughing out chucks of broken
English - how he grunted out a week's worth of grime
hurling ballincas down the pressed dirt court,
a sweaty wisp of gray hair wagging from his forehead,
"This is how the world turns. You work hard You practice."
I hear his claim as we climbed the steps of the Stadium,
higher, into the cheap seats, slapping the flat of this hand
against a girder, "I built this, Buddy."

But mostly I hear how he'd catch
what was left of his breath after Saturday's keep-busy chores,
pouring out that one, long, tall, cold beer
that Grandma allowed him, and holding it aloft,
the bubbles golden as the hayfields above the Srednevas.
He'd savor it down before taking up the last task
of his day off, cleaning the cage,
letting Snowball, canary like the ones once used
to test coal mines for poison air, flap clumsily free
around the living room, crapping on
the plastic-covered davenport and easy chairs
they only sat in twice a year.

And I'm still breathing, Grandpa, the day you took me
down the basement to the cool floor to find out
what was wrong. "C'mon, Snowball, fly, C'mon fly."
The bird splayed out on the same linoleum
where they found you, next to your iron lung,
where Grandma mopped for weeks afterwards,

pointing with arthritic fingers, "See there,
there's where he fell and bumped his head.
See the specks of blood." She can't work out.
One fine morning when my work is done,
I'm gonna fly away home,
"C'mon Snowball, fly. Fly."

Aesthetics and Strategy of the Poetry Slam
Daniel S. Solis

It's impossible to discuss all the aspects of slam strategy. Slam strategy is so many different things, from aesthetics to numbers, from getting a feel for what the crowd wants to getting a feel for what the spirits want to simply being true to yourself at the moment you begin performing a poem for an audience. Here's a brief overview of my general poetry slam strategy philosophy and some specific things concerning individual and team slam strategies.

At its most elemental and universal, slam strategy is nothing more than an excursion into aesthetics. Poem selection is like deciding where to hang a painting in a room for greatest effect, or what music to play at a party. It's like a conductor choosing a symphony program or a band hashing out a set list. The common goal is to connect with the audience in the deepest possible way. So too, the slam poet is looking for that soul deep connection. There is no one right way to accomplish this.

Extremes do exist when it comes to slam strategy. Some choose the strategy of no strategy (yes, that is also a strategy) relying on intuition, the subconscious, and the magic of the muse to connect them to the audience. Others are so concerned with analyzing a specific situation that they leave no room for spontaneity or risk-taking. Perhaps the most effective strategy lies somewhere between these two extremes. Create a plan for a specific slam, leaving room to change that plan on the fly, according to what intuition, the subconscious, and the magic of the moment tell you. In other words, be flexible.

Achieve maximum flexibility through exhaustive preparation. Memorize your slam repertoire, it helps connect you with the audience and you don't have to worry about losing your book bag. Make sure your poems are under three minutes, work with a stopwatch. Remember to check the room for acoustics and lighting, you don't want to go off the mic and into the audience with your performance if you'll be in the dark or if the room is acoustically dead. Know the structure of the specific slam you're competing in - if you're unsure of the number of rounds or other details, ask the host or house manager, that's their job. Finally have fun, there is no point in slamming if you're not enjoying yourself.

Individual Slamming

The most difficult task in any slam is going first. Be prepared for this unfortunate circumstance. Decide beforehand what poem you'll do if you draw the first slot. It should be a poem that you're comfortable with and that you feel is a real showstopper. If you perform the poem to the best of your ability, if you rock the house, you've done three things: you've set the bar at a high level for the next poets; you've captured the energy in the room; and you've endeared yourself to audience and judges. Also, deciding on your poem beforehand relieves you of making the stressful decision when you draw the number 1. The decision's been made and you simply go with it.

If you don't have to worry about what poems you're going to do, you are freed up to concentrate on performing the poem and connecting with the audience. This freedom can be achieved by pre-scripting the poems you are going to perform on a particular night at a particular slam. In other words, decide what poems you might do in various situations. Script a couple poems for the second to fourth rounds, a couple for the fifth to eighth rounds, etc. Plan on doing different kinds of poems in an evening: personal, political, humorous. The audience and judges will almost always appreciate diversity in a poet's work.

If you don't have to go first in the first round, then consider your first poem an introductory poem. This poem is how you tell the audience and judges hello — come off too strong and you might make them withdraw from the rest of your work; come off too light and they might dismiss you as fluff. There is obviously a fine line here. Flash your poetic fire but don't burn them, but don't leave them lukewarm. The poem you choose to accomplish this is a very personal decision. I've seen and been in slams where the crowd was won over by a poet's first poem and even if the poet was not as strong later in the evening the judges still choose that individual as their favorite. Conversely, I've seen slams where a good poet, despite a brilliant late round performance, was unable to overcome the stigma of an early round stumble. Keep in mind there are exceptions to all this, too.

The middle round or rounds (providing you don't have to go first) should be a place to stretch a bit, perhaps doing something that challenges the audience. Or play away from your strength: if your work is primarily comedic, do something serious. This is also a good way to set yourself up for the final round. I've found that quite often an audience will appreciate the shift in gears and subject matter. Obviously, one of the keys is to have a large, diverse repertoire. Good slamming starts with good writing.

The final round of a slam is the place to unload your best and most powerful performance poems. Whatever you have to give an audience should be given in that final round. Leave it all on stage. If you feel that you have more than one poem of an extremely high caliber, choose the one you are closest to at the time. It doesn't even necessarily mean the poem has to be dark and serious, if you feel your power lies in comedy or in a love poem then do that. (Not that you can't be serious about love or comedy.) The question of what to do in the last round of a slam was best summed up by Buddy Ray McNiece during the individual semifinals at the '92 Nationals in Boston, as he took me by the shoulders, looked in my eyes, and said, "Show 'em who you are, man. Just show 'em who you are."

Team Slamming

Being a part of a poetry slam team can be a magical, unforgettable experience. While it can also be less than incredible, let's focus on the positive aspects of the team experience and how it relates to strategy.

As a member of a team you have the responsibility of knowing your teammates and their slam repertoires. This will help you determine not only what poem might be best in a given situation, but what the demeanor and response of your teammates might be in that situation. A good coach will get to know her team inside and out, both in terms of temperament and repertoire. Some people feed off of pressure, some do better without it. Knowing these things will better enable you to map out your strategy prior to a bout of competitive poetry slamming.

Going first in the first rotation of a team bout is just as difficult, if not more so, than going first in an individual slam. The member of your team that goes first should be totally without fear. I will refer to this person as the 'point person' from here on out. The job of this person is three-fold: capture the energy in the room, stake their team a lead in the first rotation, and make it difficult for the proceeding poets to match their energy. It's a difficult job, and not for everyone. The ideal point person is not only fearless, but also perhaps a little crazy.

Going last in a bout can be just as difficult as going first. The job of this poet can be very difficult, especially if their team is behind going into the last rotation. Or not so difficult, as in protecting a lead that their team built in previous rounds. Ending with a group poem can be advantageous, especially in a close bout where you know the other team has a very strong poet that they are saving for the last rotation. Many different nicknames are used for the poet that goes up for their team in the last rotation of a slam: the closer, the hammer, the clean-up hitter.

The second and third rounds, or middle rounds, are just as crucial. These are the rounds where you can help your team build its lead or play catch-up. If considerably behind in the match you might want to do the explosive group poem you were saving for the last rotation. If the judges are giving high scores to politically charged work and you have a poet who was planning to do a comedic piece but also has powerful political poems, you might want to consider changing your strategy and go with a political poem. The specific situations are too many to anticipate, so the key to middle round adjustments are to pay attention and *be flexible*. Thankfully, there will be times when your original strategy will work throughout the bout.

The rotation of rounds in a bout is something everyone on a team should not only be familiar with, but should be able to recite from memory. The current rule for a 3-team rotation in a bout at a National Poetry Slam will, I'm sure, someday change, but for now it looks like this (with A, B, C representing three different teams)-

Round 1: A-B-C
Round 2: B-C-A
Round 3: C-A-B
Round 4: A-B-C

Which team goes first is decided on by a random draw

immediately proceeding the bout in question. There are twelve poems in a bout (three teams, with four members per team each performing once). Knowing the rotation and where your poems fall in a bout is important for two main reasons, so that you won't be caught off guard when it is your turn to go up on stage, and so that you can fine tune your strategy for a given bout. It will also make it easier to become familiar with what I refer to as "natural sets" and "resonance". We will get into natural sets first. A natural set is a place where the poems of a given team are only one poem apart. For example:

Team A has poems in the 1st, 5th, 7th, and 9th slots.
   Their natural set is 5-7-9.
Team B has poems in the 2nd, 4th, 8th, and 10th, slots.
   Team B has two natural sets, 2-4 and 8-10.
Team C has poems in the 3rd, 5th, 7th and 12th slots.
   Their natural set is 3-5-7.

The natural set is important in relation to 'resonance'. Resonance, as I use it here, is simply the way certain poems relate to and reverberate off of one another. While it's true that in a natural set the poems are separated by a poem and the accompanying scores, etc., but it's still possible to have those poems resonate off. For instance, a poem about the circus in the 5th slot and a poem about a runaway elephant in the 7th slot would resonate well, and the poet in the 7th round would probably get a higher score than the 5th round poet - this would obviously benefit the team. How a team's individual poems relate to and enhance each other in terms of style and content is a very complex and personal matter that deserves exploration by the individuals comprising the team. A good test is to perform a poem in rehearsal, then immediately perform the poem that may work best in following. Your instinct should tell you if the resonance is there or not. Remember that there's a difference between poems that resonate and poems that are similar.

These are very basic slam strategies. They don't guarantee victory, but they may help you do well consistently in the slams. Some might say that all this strategy is simply a lot of pandering to the judges. Not true! If a poem is written from a sincere place and performed with heart, that can never be pandering. Learning the best time and place to drop a specific poem on a specific audience is at the heart of all good slam strategy. Sometimes good slam strategy is to give the audience something they didn't know they needed until they've heard it. Sometimes it's aesthetic deduction, sometimes it's angelic inspiration, but it is always being true to yourself, your teammates, your muse, and your art.

Bring Them Back!
Lisa King

i want to wash myself clean in the blood of saints
the unknown martyrs
the innocent young
i want to swim in their blood and piss
to show them that i am not afraid
of the bodily fluids
that have become the poison of my generation

i would roll in the semen of a thousand dead brothers
i will tongue kiss a million prostitutes
drawing the last drop of saliva from behind rotting teeth
i will suck blood out of the syringes of every dusty junkie
i would stitch my skin onto all the quilts
that stretch from here to washington d.c.

just to hear sylvester sing again
to see a new mapplethorpe photo
to watch arthur ashe march in the streets
with haitian refugees
to know steven lawrence's laugh
as we lift a six-pack from a party

to bring back rock hudson
so he can piss on ronald reagan
and make that motherfucker remember
that he is personally responsible
for the deaths of tens of thousands

to bring back liberace
so he can shove a crystal candelabrum up george bush's ass
until that bastard screams

i'm racist and homophobic
and that's why i did nothing about AIDS

i would do all this and more
just to slam the door on this insidious disease
so i can stop
watching my friends die
so bigots disguised as religious leaders will stop
claiming to know the truth about AIDS

the truth about AIDS is
if jesus were here today his blood would be tainted
and you would call him
unclean
jerry falwell
you would call him
enemy
pat robertson
you would both try to raise money
to buy the nails

Diving Into Murky Water
Horehound Stillpoint

i'm in love and i'm totally fucked
back in the soup after all these years
after a flood of bodily fluids that lasted for a decade
history now washes over me in wave after wave after wave
at 35, i met a 19 year old
he dished me up cracklin duck and cream of asparagus
then broke my heart as completely as if it were a crystal vase
tumbling off a mantelpiece
it was all so easy for him
he was an earthquake from the get go
he realigned my tectonic plates
with a smile from the bottom of the earth
and a hard-on that shook my foundations
taking the stress off a crack that had been needing release for
generations

at 39, i met a 22 year old
he cooked me chicken soup
then trashed my heart like a sewage disposal plant
unfortunate metaphors littered our affair like
     cheap confetti at office parties on new year's eve
i just couldn't get it out of my hair
even months later, a perfect pink round dot shows up inside a
shoe
  reminding me of what a fool i made of myself
there were others, too
it's taken years to collect all the pieces of my heart
dust off that filthy old self esteem
snatch my spirit out of that hole in the ground
it's taken years to convince my super stringy center that i am
        not shit
    i do not need to be reprocessed at the mill
that it all goes into the soup
i am not only OK, i am tasty
i am rich and aromatic and well seasoned and earthy
complex and healthy and thick
then (now) at 47, i fall in love with a 23 year old
and fuck me, i am not a hearty winter-warming man-handling
stew
but i am in the soup. . . again
    like a limp overcooked out of place carrot
love is not the same at 47 as it is at 23
his love is like water out of a firehouse
it has force, direction, purpose
it can blast through walls
it fills my mouth and shuts me up and slams me off my feet
my love is like a waterfall months after the rains have stopped
a crystalline trickle
light and sad and always yielding
at 47 everything i got is yielding to gravity
at 23, it's all about liftoff
he writes me every day from el salvador
i'm drowning in his email, except that he keeps lifting me up
it's a deluge of love
i'm flailing around with everything i've got
    (yielding to gravity)

everything i've ever learned is a flotation device
breathing is a flotation device
writing is a flotation device
my blue iMac is a flotation device
   (who ever imagined that it would be a lifeline to a young gay
    man in el salvador - i thought it would be too heavy with
    gay porn pics to float)
friends are lifesavers, but they got their own rocky boats
i'm keeping my head above water
   (while tits and ass are yielding to the undertow)
i wanna go to the beach with him
   he called me from san salvador to tell me he is going
    to the beach with a friend
i wanted to climb through the phone and kiss his neck
it's impossible: he's a generation and a continent away
his best friend said: 'i can tell you fell in love in the states
is she beautiful and nice?'
he asks if it's all right if i am a nice italian girl as far as his friends
and family are concerned
i say, i'll have big pink round titties for you
i'll have thick thighs and rich juices and you can call me gina
i'd do anything for him
he says he'd rather i be amy
he says i can't imagine how hard it is for him to be in el salvador
- and he's right: i can't
i can only love him and write him and use the power of poetry to
reconceptualize what would otherwise be an intolerable situation
if you saw him, smelled him, heard him, kissed him, talked with
him in the park, visited a museum with him, wrote letters back
and forth with him, if you ever had the pleasure & the honor of
diving between his legs
   (lord, throw me a lifeline here, i'm sinking fast)
you'd understand why
i give up
there's no end to what he's pouring out
and no way to resist a current so strong
there's no point in dog-paddling in the middle of the ocean
i'm doomed and i'm fucked and it's impossible, but hand in hand
we are drowning and rising together
drowning and rising at the same time

cause love at 47 is the same as love at 23
i'm going under
watch me dive

Savanna
Ken Hunt
for everyone who has been tested for hiv

This blood which is being
drawn for the test is not
familiar blood: like watching
your closest friend go mad,
you don't quite know
the exact nature of the change.
It is the vehicle
which has allowed me
to pass through all
these situations which have led
me to this clinic
where I give only my first name.
As the needle goes in
it makes a prick like every
laser light beam that hit
me square in the eyes
as I lived the accidental,
the ironic,
the physical life.

And these veins which yield
the sample are unfamiliar interstates,
the construction project
everyone forgot about,
prone to inducing the spill
of cargo. Careful, I tell
the clinician, I've been bruising
more easily lately
and I don't know why.
This is a bald-faced lie.
I want to say further, at night

I lie awake listening to the traffic
roar and gurgle inside me,
gridlock inside the skull.
Perhaps that is why all this
has come to pass:
to cut the noise,
decongest,
relax.

And the regimen to come,
I know it already:
Cut the misbehavior, stay
at home for a couple weeks
with herbal tea and the everyday
pressure of waiting. Eat healthy,
just in case, take vitamins,
and (you should have
done this already) stop smoking.
Concentrate on work and find
the Fox station which broadcasts
reruns of *The Simpsons*
three times a day.

And the voices, they will be there too,
figures from memory that do not
merit the dignity of being
called ghosts:
C'mon, Ken,
one more vodka and Coke,
one more shot of Jaegermeister,
one more joint,
one more popper,
one more hit of X,
one more line of speed,
one more —

How many of us stumbled through high school
singing along with the Violent Femmes,
"Just One Kiss,"
and imagined it would come down to this?

As the needle is withdrawn
I rise above my body and watch it
unfold into a landscape
untouched by human works.
Savanna. Plains covered in tall,
reedy grasses. First the field mice come,
and then the grass snakes,
and then the gazelles and giraffes,
the wildebeests, and needless to say
the lions and tigers,
and finally the elephants.
Birds of prey circle, dive,
kamikaze contact with the earth.
I watch them progress in waves
until I realize it's an exodus,
that the fires have started,
and I am jarred back to my body to feel
hundreds of thousands of panicking
hooves and paws and wings
storming over every square inch of my skin.
I'm pinned down and suffocating. No
I bolt up in the clinic
chair to call out to anyone
I love enough to have hear me:
I refuse to become one of those friends
you will have to bury.

But the fact is,
my body is a landscape
and I don't know what lives there.

Anaconda, a kaddish
Brenda Moossy

It might have been you in that dream,
piloting that white convertible
like a landlocked plane over the Austin hills.
You, straddling the white line at 3 a.m.,
screaming "DO YOU LOVE ME?"

The wind sending your words
like a banner behind you.

It must have been me sitting buck-naked
on the rolled up top, my arms flung out,
my legs spread wide, feet looped behind the seat.
It was safety from flying in the face of the sky
each time there was a dip in the Bee Caves Road.

Anaconda rolls like water, *boiling*

I used to wonder:
Why you liked to roll with me in the bone yard.
Why the scent of pine and rose
and honeysuckle sent you coring deep
through my flesh like a burrowing mole
looking for the sweetest root.
How you never noticed that I shivered
in the heat of summer when you parted my legs,
that the scent of decay preceded you
pushing to my womb before you
leaving a layer of death, salting the soil.

I used to wonder how the sight of me, rocking
into cold marble, arms grasping
the monuments, and bleeding on red granite,
could make you weep,
make you cradle me,
rock me, singing,
"Baby... Baby... Baby"

I have opened like a bowl for you.
I have split my skin like a wet, ripe husk:
muskmelon orange, tomato red,
sweet warm pulp, blood purple.
I have moved aside, leaving you room
to crawl inside, my skin a shell.
I have said,
in jagged whisper,
"Do you love me?"

My words fall down my mouth
like pebbles down a well.

there is no peace
there is no peace
there is no peace

Anaconda rolls like water, boiling.
Coils loop around my ankles,
a living tattoo that slips between my thighs,
curls up my spine
squeezes fat from tissue
and marrow from my bone.
Anaconda, stealthy thief,
you steal my sleep like thunder.

Ocean Poem
Matthew John Conley

The world wished us good night & we were the ocean &
   we got it right
&the moonlight lay still upon our faces
in so many drops of water & we
lay low &
deep &
sleeping &
smiles broke over
our lips like
the slow river upon
the rocks & our eyes
rolled & swelled & reached
out towards the shoreline
the pull of the moon
& our dreams lay still beneath
the stars & you dove right
in & made your way deep
down to mossy skin & then
rose to the surface to shake the salt
water out of your hair & you looked to

the shoreline & saw me
sleeping there & you
raised your face to the moon
which lay broken in pieces upon
your cheeks & forehead & suddenly
I was beneath you & you ran
your arms & legs through & around me
& your smile broke over
your lips like a slow river upon
the rocks & we
were a million fish
wriggling in a million oceans &
you & I were an ocean poem
if there is such a thing.

Night Shift
Carl Hanni

Stone blue at midnight
she waits for the 6:00 a.m.
nervously killing time
in an all-night diner
watching the trains sidle in
trading small talk like baseball cards
mixing pathos with perfume
marking time with cups of coffee.

Outside, the denizens of the night pass by
silent, inscrutable, veiled in dark purpose
their footfalls echo dimly
and their shadows stretch and gloom
down glassy, sullen streets
streets full of dread and longing
a knife, or a kiss unfolding
on every cracked, weathered corner.

In some distant yards
the trains shift and sigh
—chug a lug—

then pick up speed
hurtling past the city's dark rim
courting heaven at every bend
the distant dawn a cigarette
on the lips of her sad-eyed man.

Big Andre
DJ Renegade

Friday night
    trying to flag a cab
    to the club
Holding the headphones
    and a crate of records
A black Lexus rolls up
    with five-star silver rims
A tinted window open
    like an eyelid
Funky rhythms float out
    like incense
What's up, need a ride?
    I nod
The door pops open
    like a mouth
The ride has the aroma
    of expensive leather
Dre sips the lips of a Heineken
    Want one?
I shake my head
    His girl laughs
    inspects her nails
Gold rings smile
    on every finger
The car springs from the curb like a cat
    a baby picture swings
    from the rear dark view
Yo, you still reading them books?
    I nod
    Fifth St. leans left abandoned buildings rush by

The light ahead revolves to red
          A dude in a dirty shirt
          Wipes the windshield
Yo, chill
          Dre kicks him a $5
          From a knot as big as a fist
The light changes its mind
          Dre starts rapping about
          how ruthless the strip is getting
How young boys
          is trying to creep up
Say his Lexus
          got bulletproof glass
          steel plates on the door
          can do 55 on four flats
He pulls up
          in the back of the club
Lean to lower the volume
          catches the meaning
          of my T-shirt in the mirror
Something appears in his eyes
          a hand disappears under the seat
          come out with a chrome .45
Y'all niggas kill me with all the blackness bullshit
          Mother Fuck Africa and some naked niggas
          running through the bush with bones in they noses
He waves the pistol
          as the flag of his country
His girl stares
          out the window
The moon covers its face
          with a cloud
Fuck all that shit, you know what I'm saying
          the only color that matters in America is green
He holds up two white rocks
          they shiver in his hand
He shakes them like dice
          they rattle like the bones
          of a very skinny man
Laughter shatters

the pain of silence
Some of the laughs swirl in the air
      like cigarette smoke
Some curl against the windows
      looking for a way
        out.

Ali
Michael R. Brown

I
Five inches shorter than his fighting height,
broad burnished face a mask with soft eyes,
hands like wood,
he was so tired when we shook he didn't see me.
The eleven-year-old next in line hung back
while his parents pushed him on.
Why shake a robot's hand?
He took a hesitant step.
Two quick jabs, Ali shuffle, eyes ablaze,
the bronze one burned seven feet tall,
fierce, playful, fast, lethal and laughing.
The kid would have fallen over backward
if his parents hadn't caught him.
Ali slowed, smiled, shook a hand,
and sank into himself.

II
"What was the most important thing you ever did?"
"Change my name."
A car salesman named Mohamed Ali
told me it's a common name.
Michael Brown ran the gambling at Foxwoods.
Michael Brown wrote the book on the Love Canal.
Michael Brown handles Canadian sales for Labatt's.
Michael Brown pitched for the Giants,
tackled for the Chiefs, played forward for somebody,
runs the Bengals operations.

Michael Brown can be anybody,
but even if I changed my name,
I couldn't be Muhammad Ali.

III
We look at him like Han Solo frozen by Jabba the Hut,
alive. . . but not quite,
slow, struggling to speak,
so easy to defeat.
Sonny Liston thought that once.
Smokin' Joe did, too.
Foreman had him beat before the fight.
Nixon had him down until he was out.
Now who's standing in the ring?
Yes, Parkinson's has him on the ropes,
but it's rope-a-dope time again,
using immobility to wear his opponent down,
learning to counter punches in brief flurries kids see.

If we get lulled into thinking once again,
yeah, the Greatest, but he can't beat. . .
the brash kid with the loose lip,
the ex-con tired old champ,
just when you counted him out,
the tiger will toss huge wooden paws in our eyes,
our own hands ineffectual,
our minds too surprised to react,
our ease arrested by all that passion,
our names meaningless next to his,
a steady burning in his eyes,
fire stoked by fury to excel,
flaring again in wordless beauty,
"I am the greatest."
Using a torch to light the Olympic flame
was merely being polite.

Big Rich Kowalski
Marty Evans

Rich Kowalski was a big, mean, hard-headed
Pollack from the neighborhoods
on the South side of Chicago.
He drank shots of Jack like water
didn't take shit from no motherfucker
and had the scars to prove it.
He was an ex-Marine
had fought in Vietnam
and never quite came
all the way home.

Rich lost a part of himself
serving as a sniper
in the Mekong Delta fighting
for God, flag, democracy
and the stockholders of
Bell Helicopter, McDonnell Douglas,
and General Dynamics.

He didn't like or trust me much
when I first signed on at the factory.
He thought I was there to steal his job.
Got so bad we nearly came to blows
but after that, we were buddies.

Rich would tell me Vietnam stories
when we drank saying how "all that
Hollywood movie shit about how
they made night vision look was total crap.
Because real infrared rifle scopes
made your night target
look just like purple haze.

He told me another tale once about
being overrun by the Vietcong and
stuck in a foxhole for two days with
a dead kid from Kentucky. Rich said

he didn't' make friends no more after that.
Wasn't any point.

I used to pick him up on Saturdays from prison
to take him to our job for his work release.
Rich was doing time for manslaughter
where he killed a young couple with his car driving
under the influence of bourbon and downers.
I sometimes think of Rich and the young
couple he killed as casualties of the patriot
machinery which teaches a seventeen-year-
old kid how to kill.

Rich, you see, had barely
made it out of the ninth grade.
I taught him words some, some spelling and
how sentences went together. He bought
the beer we drank in the tool crib.
I drank to catch a buzz.
Rich drank to wash away his shame.

One late night shift we slipped into the rail yard
to take a smoke break where we watched an old
battle scarred tomcat out prowling for rats.
Rich surprised me with a cat story
rather than another Vietnam tale.

He told how he was coming home drunk from downtown
one night when he came upon an old tomcat which let him
scratch its ears but ran from him the next day when he was sober.
He says "It's like that damn cat knew we was both out on the night
having fun and trying to get laid."

Five years later in Oklahoma the same thing happened to me.
I was in stumbling home drunk from a late night party
when I came upon an old tomcat under the street lamp.
I thought my mind was maybe tripping from the booze,
but that damn cat seemed to smile at me.
I thought of Rich instantly. Missed him.
Tried to call the next day but couldn't find his number

in Chicago information. I called our former boss.
He told me Rich had been killed
a year earlier in a car wreck.
He hadn't been drinking though,
just going home from work.
Big Rich Kawalski, distant guy,
not always friendly, hard to get to know.
Big Rich Kawalski, tattooed patron saint
of soldiers in firefights with jammed M-16 rifles.
Big Rich Kawalski, guardian angel of tomcats and
me on hot summer nights when I foolishly drank too
much and got behind the wheel.

Throb
Dayvid Figler

In the night.

Still, asphalt puddles reflect-
ing street light poles.
Traffic signal
glares along shimmer wet ground.

In the night.

At that
sudden when the ambulance siren
is first heard, the see the flashing red and blue lights--

I pull over as far to the right as I can.

Eyes narrow upon the
red blue red.
Hot white beating in the middle.
Coming closer. Getting larger than
appears in the side-view mirror.
The red blue red blue
hot white hot white
sirens horns flash speed
spin lights --

It reminds me
an awful lot
of
disco.
Real disco. Serious dis-co.
When people were
serious serious about
Sansabelt slacks and matching vests.
When people hunted
   and gathered
every available species
   and genus
of polyester off the racks of the hometown J.C. Penney's with a
vengeance

(the higher the flammability --
   the better the bargain)

The masses,
at night, draping their
bodies without the
slightest hint of irony.

They bought
chains and cocaine and did the allegedly
38 different variations
of the Hustle under
a shiny ball
and a red light
and a blue light
and a siren
and a horn

Red light blue light red light blue light
into a
Donna Summer groooove --
                  Looking for some hot stuff baby this evening
                  I need some hot stuff baby tonight (hoo hoo)

I open my eyes and I am

inside the ambulance.
It is dimly lit.
The sickly sweet smell of fog machine rises through the air.
A strobe goes off-on, off-on (that's how strobe lights work).
The paramedics are doing the Robot.

One shouts, "He's got no pulse!"
        "Oh, no... not I, I will survive!"
The other slaps white Air Hockey paddles
    together like tambourines... "CLEEEEEEEEEEAR!"

    "LOOK OUT FOR MY MEDALLIOOOOOOOOOONS!"

And the ambulance jets by --
Is there someone
dead in there or is the driver just hungry?

Either way, better them than me.

        That's the way (uh-huh uh-huh)

Toot toot.
    Aaaaaaaaah.
        Beep beep.

Motor Red, Motor White, Motor Blue
Phil West

Work was over, and I just had to go for a ride,
because you can't exactly buy stock in the sun
in late September, so I figure
I might just want to take advantage, so I

throw the briefcase in the back seat,
loosen the tie,
roll down the window,
pull on the shades,
pull on the racing gloves,
push some tunes into the tape deck,

something young and loud, some rebel guitar
raging, telling me to push that foot down,
push that foot down, keep a beat
with the speedometer needle
rising up that on-ramp and
through a herd of buffalo taking up the freeway.
And I'm saying

I don't have time to be a Sunday driver,
I don't have time to be cruising flowers,
I don't have time to be sight-seeing.

My job is job 1 and that's to push the pedal to the floor
and feel the wind and turn the tape deck up
so I can keep a beat.
And I'm forgettin' all about
the boss, and the project,
and my wife at home with the sick kid
And I'm forgettin' all about
the gas tax proposal,
and the dinosaurs gettin'
speared in the head,
and the Earth Firsters
running around sayin'
We're gonna run out. We gotta be careful.
We gotta look at alternative fuel sources.

Forgetting all about it because
No one's going to tell me what to do with my car.
No one's gonna tell me what to do with my
machine, 'cause comin' up on me
is this 17-year-old wise ass
in a decked-out Impala,
got mags and chrome everywhere,
blowing past me, passin' on the right,
got that one-fingered salute
screaming past my shotgun side
as he goes by in a brown blur
and I can't believe this guy
thinks he can do that to me.

S L A M

So I accelerate:
pop clutch third going fourth, knowing I can push
into the big O if you want,
I can hit the overdrive, I can make this thing go faster
and so I do. Needle quivering 75 80 85, and I'm catching his
rear light, I can feel it, and I catch him
glancing darting rear view mirror feeling me coming on.
I'm near 90, powerful, open hole in front of me,
truck's hitting brakes in front of him,
bluehair coastin at 50 miles an hour on his right
with a defensive driving school full of
15-year-olds swerving in front of that.
And the whole thing is mapped out
whispering in my ear saying
it's all yours, honey, oh Jesus.

Pure perfection,
now's the chance,
truck slowing, tries
to jut
left, dodge
right, nowhere
to go, I'm past his blind spot,
blazing full forward,
nothing in front of me, and I don't even have
to flip him the bird as he slips behind me
beaten like a dog
swallowing my exhaust and that kinda says it all.

And I'm feeling that knowledge,
I'm feeling it sinkin' in, and I know
there is nothing freer
than a red-blooded boy on the American road.
And I know there is nothing purer
than a red-blooded boy on the American road.
And I know there is nothing stronger
than a red-blooded boy on the American road,
and I'm staying in this left lane till
I run out of sun or run out of gas -
don't even think about
passing me.

The Wussy Boy Manifesto
Big Poppa E

My name is Eirik Ott
and I am a Wussy Boy.

It's taken me a long time to admit it.

I remember shouting in high school,
"No, Dad, I'm not gay! I'm just... sensitive.
I tried to like jet planes and hot rods
and football and Budweiser poster girls
but I never got the hang of it!
I don't know what's wrong with me..."

And then, I saw him,
there on the silver screen,
bigger than life and unafraid
of earrings and hair dye
and rejoicing in the music of The Cure
and Morrissey and Siouxsie and the Banshees,
walking loud and talking proud
my Wussy Boy icon:
Duckie in *Pretty in Pink*.

And I realized I wasn't alone.

And I looked around and saw other Wussy Boys
living large and proud of who they were:
Anthony Michael Hall, Wussy Boy;
Michael J. Fox, Wussy Boy;
and Lord God King of the Wussy Boy movement,
Matthew Broderick,
unafraid to prove to the world
that sensitive guys kick ass!

Now, I am no longer afraid
of my Wussinesss, hell no,
I am empowered by it!

When I pull up to a stoplight
and some redneck testonerone
methamphetamine jock frat boy
asshole dumb fuck
pulls up beside me
cranking his Trans Am's stereo
with power chord anthems
to big tits and date rape,
I no longer avert my gaze, hell no,
I just crank all 12 watts of my car stereo
and I rock out right to his face:
"I am human and I need to be loved
just like everybody else does!"

I am Wussy Boy, hear me roar (meow).

Bar fight? Pshaww!
You think you can take me, huh,
just because I like poetry
better than I like *Sports Illustrated*?
Well, allow me to caution you
for I am not the average, every day,
run-of-the-mill Wussy Boy you beat up
in high school, punk:
I am Wuss Core!

Don't make me get Renaissance on your ass
because I WILL write a poem about you!
A poem that will tear your psyche limb from limb,
that will expose your selfish insecurities,
that will wound you deeper and more severely
than knives and chains and gats and baseball bats
could ever hope to do.

You may see 65 inches of Wussy Boy
standing in front of you,
but my steel-toed soul
is 10-foot tall and bulletproof!

Bring the pain, punk,

beat the shit out of me!
Show everybody in this bar
what a   real   man   can do
to a shit-talking Wussy Boy like me,
but you'd better remember
that my bruises will fade,
my cuts will heal,
my scars will shrink and disappear,
but my poem
about the pitiful, small, helpless
Cock Man Oppressor you really are
will last
forever.

You Probably Can't Hook Up My VCR Either
Karen Wurl

You didn't read the instructions.
I sent you a letter, it said:
Love me.
Love me a lot.
I thought at first you
were being discreet
or subtle,
subdued,
cautious. I didn't realize
you were simply dense — See, this is the part
where you're supposed to take me in your arms,
don't you get it?
Some people don't know when to
quit but honey you
don't know when to start.

The Night Sun Rose Over Soho
Chris Brown

Cool on hot limbs
   your fingertips jazz my lips

licks off a licorice jujube.
Swapping tongues, trusts
  on a doorstep in Soho Square
    drawing the stars down
      and making a chain of cigarettes
To dream up seven moons.

Or up St. Giles, one fine night,
  guitars Django the triangle,
    Sweet Georgia,
Or waiting outside the door
  ushered in to the Presence
    conjured by night's cape:
Sun Rise, Sun Rays, Sun Ra
  trailing celestial robes
    hoisted to the piano
and sporting ceremonial headgear
  sprinkled with stars.

We took the modal elevator
  to level 13, low vibration
    of the pyramid's base
      trigonometric flights
        pass through the orbits
  The Second Stop is Jupiter
    transcending the twelfth key.
The tarnished sax, an old snake
  charm, slinking its way
    up the highest rung,
Ask Jacob or Jack,
  blowing the lid.

The incense of pow-wow tobacco
  rises nine clouds below
  chanting the planets' dance,
  the ninth chord on the horizon
And you wore Saturn's rings.

POETRY

Barefoot in the City
Lisa Buscani

You can't walk barefoot in the city.
Or you can,
if you're willing to chance...

The city covers its base
with things that stay with you,
with dog shit, with trash, with glass.

But still, you'll go when where you'll go.

They say that the foot
is the soul of the body.
No pun intended.
The center of everything is felt at the bottom.

The heat we've covered with concrete
is still with us.
We feel what's living and vital
underneath a face that would destroy us.

It's amazing what we'll do for warmth.

Pick Up
Alexis O'Hara

It's the last night of the convention. I'm all gussied up, because
no matter how fucked things get, fashion is the one thing I
always know how to do. I am leaning against the wall of the
Sons of Italy Hall in this uptight New England town. There are
cliques of American beer drinkers all around me, singing and
bonding, scouring the air for last night adventure. And
debauchery fills the air. Me, I know from debauchery. I've
already been in a darkened corner with an eager chocolate man,
swapping stories in spit. But he annoyed me. He was too drunk,
too demanding. And he hadn't been on my list of things to do,
so I walked away and found this spot against the wall of the Sons

of Italy Hall. I am trying to not look bored. I am trying to not look boring. I see you. You, who are on my list of things to do. Now I have something tangible to work on. I stare at you, burning holes first through your temple and then, aha, through your pupils. And now I have you. You are caught in my headlights. Bunny. You stare at me then turn your head around to do that teen-movie-are-you-really-looking-at-me-thing. I lower my head, my eyes nailed on yours. Yes, I am. I turn away and because I am feeling very naughty, I start to count. One one hundred, two one hundred, three one hun... You are quick as I had hoped. There you are. You are here, leaning against the wall of the Sons of Italy Hall, staring at me, closing in to speak. Your opening line will forever be mine to cherish and recall: "So, you wanna go somewhere and make out?"

Mmmm. Uh huh.

Smelling the Summer Moon
Georgia Popoff

Tuesday I smelled my mother

> A ghost of Arpege pressed to my wrist
> its obscure scent tickled my nape

>> I found the bottle hobnobbing with
>> Givenchys and Chanels in a trendy perfumery
>> Her mist became my own

Today I smelled my mother

> as the wind issued its frantic threat
> to stifle heat with thunder as the storm barged through

>> The lusty aroma of wet dust and tiger lilies
>> held her captive at the first hint of lightning
>> I still bow to such power
>> and the bouquet of its aftermath

Tomorrow I will smell her

after this night in your arms

My thighs still damp from loving you
and the musk of mornings after
she had held my father a prisoner
of her perfume

I read my new piece over the phone
My friend confesses she has no sense of smell

My fragrant poem
and her sad admission
create space in the summer night

Like a blind man asking to feel red and blue
she wants lines repeated
questioning if her memories are trapped
Her senses robbing her of ways to rub the lamp

I wonder if her hands touch
in a way other than I understand
or if sound and color are her incense

Pale consolation
I tell her there's a poem in this

I am anxious to share my mother's mist
Mingle it with moonlight

But I can't get this new scent
of nothingness
out of my head

Looking for Nice Green Sandals
Sheila Donohue

Betty threw up on the shoes of a woman working in a drugstore.
Betty threw up everything that ever came into her.

Every fucking thing that ever came into her.

People in the drugstore, silently getting sick.
Not really sick, of their own, on their own.
Just embarrassed.

The anonymous, enormous, anemone people.
The anonymous various marine people that
Attach themselves to rocks,
Suggesting flowers by their coloring and outspread tentacles.

People embarrassed but watching,
Waiting for Betty to crawl out,
Head down, anonymous like their anemone selves.
People staring.

She was through getting sick on the shoes of the drugstore
woman and
Betty just wanted to browse.
Browse around the drugstore.
Maybe buy some nice green sandals.

The Evolution of Slam Strategy
Taylor Mali

The strategy for winning a multi-round individual poetry slam
has not changed much over the years, regardless of the way each
venue structures its slams. The first poem performed should be
one that will make you the crowd favorite, something powerful
and entertaining. Once you have earned the audience's attention,
however, they will allow you — in fact, they expect you — to be
more insightful and reflective in the later rounds. Funny poets rarely
win slams on humor alone.

But team slams — such as those occurring at the National
Poetry Slam every summer—is a different beast altogether: Three
teams of four poets, reading in a different order in each of four
rotations. Team strategy (not to mention team politics) can make
or break a team in a hotly contested bout. Although the best

strategy is to perform fantastic poetry fantastically, here's a quick look at three other strategies that have been used in recent years.

The Crescendo Strategy

Old time slammers and teams with prima donna superstars still swear by this save-the-best-for-last strategy. Because the judges' scores tend to rise over the course of the bout, the last rotation is usually the highest-scoring rotation. Any poet on your team who thinks she has a shot at individual glory may insist on reading in the last rotation. If you have two such divas on your team, the other one will probably demand he read in the third rotation, thereby effectively cutting your strategic options in half. Teams that use the Crescendo strategy start with their weaker stuff and try to end with a bang. As many teams have discovered, the slam usually has been won or lost before the fourth rotation begins.

Frontloading Strategy

In recent years, a greater number of teams have paid more attention to the earlier rotations in their bouts. To quote Bill MacMillan, member of the championship Providence team in '96 and coach of the finalist Worcester team in '97, "Slams are won or lost in the first two rotations." Although this may be an oversimplification, many teams have realized the importance of building an early lead. Roger Bonair-Agard, coach of 1998's championship New York team put it this way, "You can't rely on score creep to make up a two-point deficit in the third and fourth rotations if everyone is getting 29s." In an example of solid team strategy, at the 1998 finals the New York team had four excellent poets, and led off with the one who was most capable of getting the highest score in the first rotation. By nobly demonstrating a willingness to put the team's chance of winning over his individual score, this poet relinquished his shot at individual stardom to serve his team.

Flashpoint

The most effective strategy is also the least widely used. In the Flashpoint strategy, you put your team's best piece — whether it's a group piece or an individual piece — in the rotation in which your team gets to read last. The idea is this: judges give out relatively low scores until some poet or poem gives them a compelling reason to do otherwise. All scores after that "flashpoint" tend to be higher because the judges are jazzed and have realized that giving high scores is actually fun. Everyone who follows the flashpoint poet rides on the coattails of the flashpoint's success; but if the flashpoint poet was the last poet in her rotation, then the other two teams will have to wait until the next complete rotation to start making up the difference.

To illustrate, observe how Dallas made a strategic blunder at the 1998 National Slam finals in Austin. Everyone was talking about "Super Heroes," their group piece that went on to get the only perfect score of the night — in fact, the only perfect score in the last five years of National Slam finals. The crowd was waiting for it, and the judges could tell something was up. But Dallas unwisely waited until the fourth rotation to use the piece! Why? Because they were using the Crescendo strategy. Had they used "Super Heroes" in the third rotation, when they were the last team to perform, it could have helped them more and might have enabled them to beat New York. But you learn something new at every slam.

Crazy Hunger
Lisa Hammond

Crazy Hunger
Do you know it?
The kind that drives you
to the kitchen at 3 a.m.
to the Banquet Chicken box
to chew off thawed skin
by the light of the freezer

Crazy Hunger
You know
the one that drives you
to call your first boyfriend
seven years later
to ask him what he meant
when he said what he said
that one night

Crazy Hunger
And if you feed it
It will grow!

Mango Pantoum
Eve Stern
(Written after I was told the proper etiquette
for eating mangoes was naked in the bathtub)

Mangoes should be eaten naked.
You have to strip them,
take their skins off:
tongue them slow and tender.

You have to strip them:
they're as ticklish as young brides.
Tongue them slow and tender;
appreciate their new color.

They're as ticklish as young brides:
red, yellow, green, unripe.
Appreciate their new color;
tell them they're pretty.

Red, yellow, green, unripe:
mix them with lime and swallow.
Tell them they're pretty.
Tell the mangoes that you love them.

Mix with lime: and swallow.
Take their skins off,
tell the mangoes that you love them —
mangoes should be eaten. Naked.

French-Kissing Martha Stewart
Cin Salach

1.
I spend the entire morning missing you while you drive home
the only way you know and I let you go even kiss you good-bye

then cry when I imagine you coming into another sunset
without me
there to applaud or sing or steer.
I want to tell you *this is not a translation this is a collaboration*
so you can tell me what's wrong, put your hand flat on the back
of my neck
climb inside my mouth and introduce your tongue to each tooth.
It won't take long. And we have all life. Maybe then I'll know
why I feel the way I do coming into you, the way breath flies
out of my body, the way my lips egg it on "harder, faster!" like
two pouty cheerleaders
who naturally assume the whole show rests on their shiny
shoulders.

2.

Every course feeds the same sore muscle — heart, gut, kegel.
Food finds its way in then leaves again and we woo nourishment
like a lover: *Mangia, mangia, Ciao!*
You are so intensely bella when you are eating me,
I place water, salmon, religious oils at your feet to give you strength
and pray that I can be a good meal.
I want to stay conscious long enough to get the recipe.
I want to pass out. I want to skip straight to dessert.
I want more whipped cream. I want you to want seconds.

3.

It's a simple test – if the toothpick comes out clean,
the cupcakes are done. My mother taught me that.
She's not an exuberant cook, but she knows
how to end a meal. To me, a good dessert is like
a good last line: everyone remembers it the next morning.
In my mother's one-and-only cookbook, there's a yellowing quote
on the bottom of page 43: "a good hostess must put herself inside
her guest's
mouth to determine the what and when of the next course."
Empathetic cooking. Brava! Brava! In my dream,
Martha Stewart climbs inside my mouth to determine my next
course.
She is so taken with my taste, she dedicates her next book to me:
"To Cin, for helping me cook."

Wow, I think, she is a good hostess.

I'm hungry all the time.
"Let's eat!" I scream every chance I get. *Mangia! Mangia! Chow!*
The world is my dinner table.
Every guest is you.

Chinese Restaurant
Justin Chin

I thought you'd like to know what really goes on in the kitchens of Chinese restaurants.

Well, when they say, "No M.S.G.," they're lying. When they say, "Tell us how hot & spicy," they really don't give a flying lizard fuck what you tell them, there's only one recipe, and you're going to eat it. And yes, they do spit into the food of the idiot, you know the one who everybody in the restaurant can hear:

"How hot and spicy is that? Is it hot hot, or spicy hot, or chili hot, or garlic hot? It's not peppers, is it? Cos if it's too hot, I get a burning in my asshole when I shit." (Order the fucking steamed vegetables, buddy) And yes, they do laugh quite unmercifully at the fool who actually tries to follow the pictorial instructions on how to use chopsticks that's printed on the back of the chopstick wrapper. And just what the hell is Kung Pao, anyway?

In the kitchen of a Chinese restaurant they don't wash their hands much, but you already knew that. In the kitchen of a Chinese restaurant, someone is working way too hard for minimum wage but hey — it's a family thing, so it's okay and hey — it's America, where you make it if you work 12 hours a day, 7 days a week, so you can dream the American Dream, you know the one: where Diane Parkinson of *The Price Is Right* or Bob Barker of *The Price Is Right* spread it just for you. (Which one depends on your sexual orientation, No Substitutions Please. Unless, of course, you're Bi, then it's your lucky day.) Come On Down!

In the kitchen of a Chinese restaurant the waiter lives in fear of deportation, the dishwasher lives in fear of being bashed

for stealing some stinking job nobody wants, the kitchen helper
is scared to death of participating in the democratic political
process & the chef knows someone who has AIDS at home or
abroad.

From the kitchen of a Chinese restaurant I look for some
semblance of the familiar. I look for home in every bite. In the
dead spit of morning, after equal hours of "Silence=Death,"
"ACT-UP FIGHT BACK" & "What Do We Want? A Cure!
When Do We Want It? Now!" I want some friendly solace & all
I find is a lousy jerk-off, interrupted only by the 300-pound clerk
who sticks his head through the door every ten minutes to yell,
"Buy your tokens. Get into a booth or get out of here!"

I find no simple gesture can erase it all. I find a border that I
cross each day for a decent wage of self-deception: call it
optimism, call it a punch-fuck, fist-fucking the ass of the quality
of life (and it's a tight one too, baby.)

I find a pissant pleasure, a memoir of failure, cancer for
brains. & I want to go, got to go, got to find this thing called
home.

In the kitchen of a Chinese restaurant, I am queer for queer
I refuse to pass my ugliness for roses. I refuses to trade my queer
for your queer.

At this point you're probably thinking, wait a minute, all of
this wasn't in *The Joy Luck Club*; all this wasn't in the PBS
special presentation, *A Thousand Pieces of Gold*, & all of this
probably isn't in that stage production of *The Woman Warrior*,
either.

But I just thought that you should know what goes on in the
kitchens of Chinese restaurants.

Now go eat.

Artichoke
Wendi Loomis

You are the most beautiful one I have ever seen
On display so ripe and fresh,
I have to take you home.
I steam bathe you long and tediously,
but the first bite is so bittersweet wonderful

POETRY

I pause afraid.
Overcoming this,
I realize the leaves are sweeter the further down I get.

I become more cautious now,
Looking for the brown spots, holes,
dirt warning signs of pestilence.
I want so much for you to be perfect
I am frightened of going further,
Leery of the dark secrets you may hide.

Every now and again your needle point leaves
will prick my fingers,
prick my lips.
I become more cautious,
wondering: "Is it worth the trouble?"

The leaves become so tender
the further down I get,
I rush on heedless of the points grown soft
They barely scratch.
The core's heat is strong enough to slow me down again.
Patience is demanded before I can
touch you now.

When I do, I find the tiny fur-like needles
hot to touch and messy.
It takes time and care to get past them all.
So many little nuisances!

But once they're gone and my fingers are wiped clean,
I'm amazed at what I find,
The most vibrant tender delicious part,
Your heart.

Le Pain Perdu
Castadera McGee

"What's the recipe?"
Simple questions should have simple answers but this

particular one
unearthed complications

"How did you make it?"
Vadim doesn't realize what he is asking
the forces he tangles with
the knowledge he craves
the can of worms he is prying open
It is Thanksgiving Day and I am being asked
for my pedigree in culinary alchemy
my license to practice voodoo
my soul on a silver platter
my blood

"How do you make jambalaya?"
And suddenly I feel like I need to explain myself
My mind runs through possible answers
and I settle on...
"It's a secret - a family secret."
I have settled on bold-faced lies

When people find out you're from New Orleans
you are expected to work your hoodoo
and conjure a steaming cauldron of gumbo
or the savory mess of jambalaya
instantly - from thin air

I don't know that trick
My Grandma made me her apprentice
when I asked for the lesson
She tried to show me
the secret of every good pot of gumbo
- it's in the roux
The delicate balance of
flour, oil, seasoning, and a properly heated skillet
is far too volatile for inexperienced hands to mess
with
Needless to say
if my palm were read by
a bayou voodoo priestess,

in the bleak outlook of smooth skin
is where the truth could be found
I wasn't paying attention
when the lesson was given
My hands do not know calluses from two-hour vigils
on top of cutting boards,
mincing the Holy Trinity
(onions, garlic, and bell peppers),
with the rank of shrimp heads and shells
wafting from garbage bags
that will soon be filled with more carnage
My hands do not know burns
from hot flour and oil
in a trial and error effort
to prepare the perfect roux

The truth is
I stayed away from my Grandma's kitchen
except when I was surveying pots
or dishing out their contents
Why gain experience when I can go make groceries
and get instant roux mix
in a cardboard cylinder
It's so easy to be a Creole chef
when you have boxed mixes for
gumbo, red beans and rice, crawfish etoufee, dirty
rice, crab cakes and yes... jambalaya
just like the box I used
to make the batch I took
to Vadim's Thanksgiving potluck

What's so lucky about
the burning red embarrassment
of being exposed as a phony
Red like the crimson stock
of Vadim's pot of luck borscht
except he did not scan grocery store aisles
for cans or boxed mixes of a dish
he is expected to conjure
instantly - from thin air

when people find out he's from Russia
(He knows that trick)
Borscht takes better after a few days
(He learned that secret)
It has something to do
with the sugars in the pot
Vadim's hands know a thing or two about borscht

If I posed the same question,
"What's the recipe?"
Vadim could make me his apprentice
show me the secret
or
he could be really clever
preserve his "family secret"
and give me my cooking lesson
while speaking Russian so
I couldn't understand

We only spoke English in my home
so despite having a Creole-peppered patois
the language is lost in me
I say "beaucoup" - a lot
I call my godfather "parrain"
A bit of advice... to avoid adventurous Creole dining
one should learn the difference between
"mirliton" and "caquane"
but you can't go wrong with a
"beignet" and "café au lait"
for dessert

It hurts sometimes
to be so close to
having a second language
to use when English fails
as it so often does
When someone pissed me off
I could mutter something in Creole
wiggle my hands in front of their face
have them thinking I'm throwing a hex -

my own pseudo voodoo
I sometimes think that if I knew Creole
I wouldn't feel so distant
from the folks I see in
yellowed and tattered photos
when I'm told that they are family
I would be linked to my great-great-great
so many times great Grandmother
who had an apprentice in the kitchen
who imparted secrets
who defiantly shook her hands
in the face of her white rapist
in a desperate effort
to ward off the attack
Her hex was real

Here's a little "lagniappe"...
gumbo tastes like shit after a few days
something sours in the pot
perishable
like your roots
lost
like your language
forgotten
like your memory of
where you came from
if you are too busy not paying attention
when lessons are given
and secrets are told
It leaves too much room for misconceptions
When allowed
I consider myself lucky that
I can clear up a few

Creole and Cajun
are not the same
For some Creole is a savory cultural mess of
Acadian French, Spanish, and African cultures
For others it is a cultural loophole,
a way for light-skinned Black folks to "pase blanc"

or otherwise deny their African origins
That's what Grandma said
despite having skin as fair as some white folks
That's what Grandma said
in English peppered with Creole
Like I said before
complications

And while someone in New Orleans is saying
"Laissez les bon temps passer"
I'm over here in San Jose
having the worst time
keeping my ruse from crumbling
I feel like the biggest fraud
lying to Vadim
telling him that the recipe for my jambalaya
is a secret,
a family secret
It's not -
it's a mystery

Your Father Says You Are Beautiful
Faith Vicinanza
(for Justin Michael Arroyo - born July 22, 1996)

Her tan legs weary from the weight of you
now stretch to breaking as she heaves and trembles
and turns in her pain. We wait the hours
she pushes, strains, to bear you incomplete.

Your father will say, even after they
open you sideways, far wider than you
opened your mother, that you're beautiful.
Your father, my son, her lover, my son,

will say it again, again and again,
intending you to life, to the living.
It is an incantation meant to fill in the spaces
where dreams should have gone, fill in the chasm
in uncertain hearts, provide some relief

from the scalpel edged moment to moment
considerations. We are all afraid.
Mother's breast replaced by i.v. tubes in

and catheter out, your arched back aching
for the seashell nook of your mother's arms.
The familiar beat of your mother's heart
replaced by the beat of machinery.

We are all afraid, and your father says
in early morning dim hospital room
and in late hours, that you're beautiful,
you are beautiful, and you are,

you are.

Mirage
Da Boogie Man

i held my son for the first time in four years
he was feather lite as a dream
when i put him down
waved him back
and threw him his first football
passed
him
in a race that moved as swift
as a
premonition
about going
to the amusement
parked
the car
as his eyes lit up
like christmas lights
he's never seen at my
house
has
an empty bedroom

with his
name
is gabriel
and this is his picture
at one month
before
i didn't see him
for two years
when i picked him up
in a
memory
about a
premonition
doesn't fill my arms
like my
son
doesn't know me
anymore
time apart
from him will suffocate me
and i'm not
ready
to
die

Tour
Genevieve Van Cleve

How often do poets get flown overseas to do anything but get the fuck out of wherever they're from? And to Europe no less? Poetry is the roundworm on the food chain of the arts - to admit to a life of poetry is paramount to admitting to living in your parent's basement, swallowing gallons of Nyquil to make the bad voices go away. "Hey everyone, I'm a crazy loner, who has a taste for Oedipus and NyQuil. Hey, where ya' goin'?"

Well, not this time, thanks to the Danish government and Janus Kodal. Myself and five of my poetry (spoken word for those in the know) sisters were flown to, booked in, paid for, and put up in Copenhagen, Arhous, and London to perform our work. We did four shows in four days, and then were sent back to our homes, our own turf. It was a short trip, but none of those Danes, or us, or even those English will every forget it; we were Amazons on Tour. Here's the story.

I'm two days outside of leaving for a trip I'd been looking forward to for months and I can't stop making furtive trips to the can or sweating. Travel makes me nervous. Performing makes me nervous. Facing the country that houses my ex-fiancé makes me nervous. My last trip to Europe had been pretty horrible. Note to self: Do not go 3,000 miles to get engaged to an asshole. If you must get married to an asshole, do it at home. The foundation for my most recent European vacation was laid out by my last trip. I tagged along to Copenhagen with a Bristol UK contingent of poets who performed at an English language festival. Our host, Janus Kodal, was warm, generous, and above all interested in bringing the fast and loose world of spoken word to his content, well-mannered Danish brethren. I convinced Janus to come scout a group of American poets to make the journey to Copenhagen. He chose all women: National Poetry Slam champions and professional writers and performers — a very talented group of artists. Our band of Amazons included Staceyann Chin from New York City; Noel Jones, also from the Big Apple; Melinda Corazon Foley from Santa Cruz; Kim Holzer from Chicago; Ariana Waynes from San Francisco; and me.

The promo poster on the door to our first gig pointed out, "You've Never Heard Women Talk Like This Before." We arrived in Copenhagen, checked in to our hotel, slept, changed and went to the first gig. It was a kind of "meet and greet" affair - we were giving the audience a teaser of our work and us before the big show the next evening. We did our thing, small sets of one or two poems each and then, snacks and drinks with the audience. The audience was intrigued with our work and style and we were surprised, I think, at the power and depth of each of our performances.

Some of the girls went back to battle with jet lag, I went out with Noel, an ex-pat named Michael, and a couple of Danes. I asked them to take us to the sketchiest disco in town (Hard to do in a town with so little sketch), but we found it. Techno Techno Techno. Lager Lager Lager. And finally, a certain Danish young man and myself left the others for a hash and MDMA-induced walk around the city. I'm not exactly sure what was in that little pill, but the lake and the bridges and the buildings were singing gracefully, lighting up the night. My Danish friend was a perfect gentleman as I talked and talked and talked and just told him everything. I hadn't talked to a man that I didn't know or wasn't related to in ages. I was, and still am, on a six-month probation from men. Too many bad choices and not enough love can wear a girl out. So, I had a lot to say. He listened, laughed, pointed out the cool historical points of Copenhagen. We ended up in the Jazz Club of Copenhagen at 4 a.m. for sodas and warmth.

The next morning came and went as I was coming down. We made a quick trip to Christiania, an anarchist neighborhood in the middle of the city that happens to have open-air hash markets —I can't tell you how nice it was to spark one up over a sandwich and a coffee without feeling like a criminal. Off to bed after lunch for a much-needed nap, and up in time for our appointment at the hairdressers. All of this really happened, you can ask the others. They had curlers and sodas waiting for us. The nice beautician lady looked at me and asked, "What do ummm?. You want me to do?" I told her, "Ma'am, make it (pointing to my short hair) big." I am, after all, from the Lone Star state, and if a girl can't rat her hair up and put on a little rouge from time to time, then what did all those feminists like Ann Richards and Liz Carpenter fight for?

The gig approached, and us girls were circling the wagons testing each other's resolve. After all, this was a poetry slam, there was prize money, a trophy, and bragging rights back home up for grabs. The audience was amazed by all of us, but particularly by Noel Jones and Stacyann Chin. They really moved the crowd to heights of excitement that the Danes haven't experienced since that messy family affair at the castle that we all read about in school a long time ago. Both of these women tackle all the big stuff: gender, history, loss, triumph, revolution, beauty, and with each word, each movement, they make you want to fight wars for them. It was their night.

I took some chances that night. I've never been one to improvise, but the moment seemed right and I had forgotten some of my lines. I went beyond what I thought were my own limits with my work. Well, after the previous night and a sore throat, I went home early and gloriously slept. We were to be on the train to Arhous, the second largest city in Denmark, by 9 a.m.

The train ride to Arhous was joyous, with lots of singing and laughing. The poor Danes on the train were packed in with a pride of loudmouthed Americans and their international entourage of rock and roll carolers. We sang every song we knew, Whitney Houston and Ethel Merman all in the same breath. When we arrived, we took it easy before the show and managed to do our own hair, although how we managed after the royal treatment in Copenhagen, I'll never know.

I was in a terrible mood when we got to the café. I hated my work, my stupid plainness, and all the fresh faces of the women around me. I felt dry, pruny, and passed it. The café provided us with a very nice meal and I began to get over myself enough to talk to the girls. The Arhous audience was a bit more subdued but they really got a kick out of the lot of us. Arianna Waynes was the belle of the ball. They loved her youthful candor and innocence. Melinda Corazon Foley really let them have it. I'm pretty sure the Arhous crowd had never heard the stories of urban decay Melinda unleashed. I believe they were confused and then grateful for her words.

Arhous is not known for its nightlife, so we called it a night after some relatively subdued drinking and dancing. I woke up before Kim, my roommate, and turned on the TV as I prepared for the next leg of the journey to London. Bam Flash Pow? It's 8 in the morning and there's porn on Danish TV - Boobs, Dicks, Vaginas? Everything.

Traveling is all weird. Time goes by very quickly, but sitting on busses, trains and planes bores me to tears and makes me claustrophobic. A bunch of strangers are sucking in all that precious filtered air. It's enough to make a girl hack folks up with a spade; thank God for Nicorette gum and ibuprofen. Further, travelling in London is as dreary as English weather. The girls and I were tired, hungry, and lost. Our escorts were friendly enough but London is seedy and there's no way of getting around that. The cab tried to rip us off, the hotel manager didn't think that towels and wake-up calls were included in the bill, and the promoter of the show guilted us out of our fee. (That's the last fucking time I perform without a contract. I don't care if I am a lowly poet, getting ripped off after we pulled off a fabulous show sucks.) However, we gave the performance of our lives that night. Deep in the bowels of a club in Islington, we gave those people a show to remember.

I'm not sure our American spoken word peers or audiences

would have recognized us that night. There was no competition, there were only our cracked, sore voices calling to the audience to see it with us, feel it with us, watch us love each other as we tore our hearts out for them. I have never felt such a deep connection with other writers, performers, or women. We were Amazons on tour, the Mermaids of Copenhagen. We were too tired that night to take it all in, too chapped at being ripped off to say good-bye properly.

Our planes and lives awaited us the next morning. I don't know if we'll all be in the same place again or work together again. I'd give anything to do it. Some of us are students, full-time performers, tech writers, temps, and future brides. Amazing that it took the Danish government and our dear friend Janus to bring us together. Thank you Denmark, we'd like to take you home with us, we'd like to take you home.

Picasso
Ellyn Maybe

I found a year that likes my body
            1921
girl sitting on a rock
Picasso painted a woman
with my thighs

walking around the museum
it hit me how Rubenesque
is not just some word
for someone who likes corned beef

there I was
naked on the edge of something
overlooking water
or was it salt

it was weird
nobody was screaming fat chick at the frame
nobody was making grieving sounds
but the girl in the painting looked sad

as though she knew
new ears were smudging
a forced liposuction
with rough acrylic

the caption said
girl sitting on rock

not woman who uses food to help cope
for the lack of empathy in her sphere

not the gyms are closed and there are
better muscles to develop

not girl one calorie away
from suicide

just flesh on a rock

her eyes dripping
questions marks onto
girl looking into a mirror

the vibrancy
the need to chew the ice cubism
till the teeth bleed
the colors so deep
they look wet

the museum guards
watch me tentatively
I lean into the paintings
I veer to the outside
to find out what Picasso
called each work

I like titles
their vocabulary of oil
the girl on the rock
whispered to me

go girl

I love museums
call me old fashioned
but I like face to face
conversations.

The Freedom
Tracy Townsend

It was just an idea
        someone thought up
    driving through a long Texas night
    heading for a cool Colorado morning
    rolling over the flat plains
flying to the peaks of the Rockies

sweating in the middle
of a sultry August night
steam coming off
a straight stretch of highway

my hags and I on our
haunches for the haul hallowed
grounds of Oklahoma left behind
someone spoke through the sticky atmosphere
- Hey, let's strip off our shirts.

so we did.

It was a bit odd-feeling at first
that part of the female anatomy
not being used to
so much open air
        unless, of course, possessors of
        abovesaid anatomy are employed as
        models or nudie dancers.

The rest of us gals keep our hooters

boobies racks jugs titties
   milk-duds chi-chis ta-tas
      and torpedoes
  bound up in nylon lycra
cotton spandex plastic and
malleable metal wire

under our clothes to prevent
jiggles wiggles and T-H-O's
otherwise known as smuggling raisins.

Smug in our satisfaction
we sat shirtless giggling in the
 swarthy soot-stained gunmetal night
     breakin' the law
     breakin' the law
at 3:30 a.m. in a red Geo Prism
pushing eighty miles an hour

careening in the car
commuting au natural
commenting on society's
expectations of women

You guys, you have it easy
you're expected to go topless
at the beach mowing the lawn
  why do you think you mow the lawn?

It's not just men, women do it too.
We all tsk-tsk sneer and make
self-righteous sly remarks at the
slightest infraction of the rules
    a low cut dress
    a stray bra strap
    or heaven forbid
    (gasp) a nipple!
So strange a concept - breasts
We were raised with Barbie
   who is probably a 38DD

yet has no nipples
As young women we were
thrown into training at the
sight of the slightest lump
    covering concealing
    enhancing enlarging
told our tits would hang to
our hips like those women in
National Geographic unless we wear the
over-the-shoulder-boulder-holder
on a semi-regular basis

The later the letter the better
movin' on up (and out)
sent up from the AAA league
to the AA's then A's B's C's and D's
    hoping one day to match the Barbie

Our society's sex symbols
are large-breasted small-hipped women
a body type I might add that isn't
found too often in the general population
without the aid of plastic surgery

either by removing from the bottom
adding to the top
or both

pieces of plastic, metal, and silicone
stuck in various parts of our body
I wonder what archeologists will think
about our culture
one thousand years from now

We sat in whirring-car silence
wishful thinking and what-iffing
moving only to put back on our shirts
at the lights of the next sleepy-small town.

Pucker
Ritah Parrish

My love is deep and penetrating. Subterranean.
Large, thick, slow, deliberate, vulgar, low, archetypical,
animalistic.
Ripe for splitting open, to be savored, enjoyed.
I am a pomegranate.

And you.
You are everything that ever was
And everything that ever shall be.
I could pray to you.
And, so it begins.

You take me in your arms and fold me like a fan.
You lead me about the room.
My body is pliant, supple.
Your hands stretch wide across my belly, self-assured.

Even your fingers are confident.

We are groveling.
Grinding.
Sinking deeper into it.
Slathering each other with it.

And, then I feel it.

It is traveling through my bowels
Like a vengeful eggplant on fire,
Violently pushing and gurgling its way through my lower
intestine.
Mocking my sensuality.

For a moment I am shaken.

How can this be? I was so careful at dinner.
Oh God, the cauliflower.
Why? On this day of all days.

S L A M

The day I wear the crown of woman.

I travel through time.
Suddenly I am 9 years old, in Sister Mercede's 4th grade class.
And Christi Ramalo, with her ample bosom and hairy upper lip,
Tells me I'm not cool enough to be in the 7-Up club.
And all my mother can say is,
"Honey, sometimes life just isn't fair."

For a moment I fantasize
Just letting it rip.
Will you liken me to some winsome peasant?
Will you love the honesty of it?

Maybe you'll think I'm earthy.

Next, I imagine standing up,
Clutching the bedpost
And proudly declaring,
"It is I, Flatula!"

Would that frighten you, my love?

My muscles tighten
And I begin to pray,
Sweet Baby Jesus
Let your light shine through me and
Neutralize this demon squash-like gas.

I feel an enormous thrust. Is it over?
You cover me with kisses and tenderly pat my thigh.
I tense up and hope for a miracle.
I whisper, "Sweet dreams, my love."
Barely able to contain the steaming monster inside me.

You begin to snore.

I press myself against the wall,
Adhering my buttocks firmly to it
And say twenty-seven

Hail Marys.

I relax for one tiny moment and it moves,
Explodes.
And I am thrown from the bed.
Dear God help me!

A loose chunk of plaster breaks from the ceiling
And flies through the air.
I try to throw myself in front of it.
I try to cheat fate.

But it is too late.
Too late my love.
The plaster chunk delivers
A cruel but swift death.

I cradle your dented head in my arms and I weep.

I weep for the cruelty of fate,
The loss of true love,
And my lack of muscle control.

I blame myself.

Romy's Poem
Dufflyn Lammers

Well hello, Fireman, you sure look fine in the morning light,
won't you show me your candy like you did last night? Come on,
Fireman, don't you want to hear me call you flamejockey,
polepappy, hot-silly-sauce, my very cherry popsicle, my fire
fuckin' daddy? Come on, baby, at least my cat calls like an
original. You better be ready to dine where you dish, because I
am a woman who won't take no for an answer. Are you ready,
Fireman? Show me you Salami! The Full Monty, the whole
schtick, the real Irish Brigade. I want to see you lift that kilt in
the clear light of day — what's this, No? Not during your parade?
What did you say? Your family could be watching? Did you think

last night you were in another world? Did you think I wasn't someone else's little girl, someone else's faithful wife? Listen up, cupcake, I've got something to ask you and I won't take no for an answer. You can call it war, or call it sex; when you hear the girls shouting: Free Willie! Show Your Dick! You know, you started it.

Didn't you and your friends get a big kick flashing me your penises while I mixed your gin and fizz? As if you were the first drunks to want to see me top free? These two boobs are prize-winning piglets, twin Pulitzers, pendulous sundials, wild wet two-story tits! But most of all, these breasts are mine. I don't need your money or your beads or your good opinion. Flattery, Fireman, is a gift, not a demand. All you offered me was an opportunity to give away what, by your judgement, is my most valuable trait. Honey, I'm a bartender and I'm used to this crap. It's bad enough you whistle and comment and pinch a girl's ass, but I am laying it down: I don't care what day it is, and I don't care what town you're in, you can't go around demanding to see tits, it's a bar, Fireman, not the third world.

And I want you all to know about the women of Afghanistan behind the cloth, their sad little mouths not allowed out for fear they will shout each other into a frenzy. A woman driving let a bit of arm show and quick as thieves a crowd had torn her from her car and stoned her to death.

And if this is a war of the sexes, Fireman, I want you to know you're in it. Don't you see, it's only different by degrees? The Taliban controls women starting with their bodies: forcing them to keep covered. As if a swatch of female skin would drive men mad. Frat boy, rednecks, and, apparently Irish firemen flown in for parades, do it shouting, "Show me your tits." As if not enough skin would drive men mad. The point is not whether or what we show, it's whose choice it is. Choice is the issue and I am the woman who won't take no for an answer. Look now, Fireman, look down on your world, look down on your pools of Viagra and Propecia, pec implants and penis pumps — this is your backlash. This is the objectification of you, this is the dissection of a man's body parts. Parts. And nothing more.

Chicks Up Front
Sara Holbrook

Before and After,
we stand separate,
stuck to the same beer-soaked floor,
fragranced, facing the same restroom mirror.
Adjusting loose hairs —
mine brown, hers purple.
Fumbling for lipsticks —
mine pink, hers black —
a color I couldn't wear anyway
since that convention of lines gathered around my mouth last
year and won't leave.
We avoid eye contact,
both of us are afraid of being carded.

Mature, I suppose, I should speak,
but what can I say to the kind of hostility
that turns hair purple and lips black?
Excuse me, I know I never pierced my nose,
but hey, I was revolting once too?
Back. Before I joined the PTA,
when wonder bras meant, "where'd I put that."
I rebelled against the government system,
the male-female system,
the corporate system, you name it.
I marched, I chanted, I demonstrated.
And when shit got passed around,
I was there, sweetheart, and I inhaled.
Does she know that tear gas
makes your nose run worse than your eyes?
Would she believe that I was a volunteer when they called
"chicks up front," because no matter
what kind of hand-to-hand combat
the helmeted authoritarians may have been
engaged in at home,
they were still hesitant to hit girls
with batons in the streets.
"CHICKS UP FRONT!" and we marched and

we marched and we marched right back home.

Where we bore the children we were not going to bring into this
  mad world, and we
brought them home to the houses we were never going to
  wallpaper
in those Laura Ashley prints
and we took jobs with the corporate mongers
we were not going to let supervise our lives,
where we skyrocketed to
middle-management positions
accepting less money
than we were never going to take anyway
and spending it on the Barbie dolls
we were not going to buy for our daughters.

And after each party
for our comings and goings
we whisked the leftovers into dust pans,
debriefing and talking each other down
from the drugs and the men
as if they were different,
resuscitating one another as women do,
mouth to mouth.

That some of those we put up front
really did get beaten down
and others now bathe themselves daily
in Prozac to maintain former freshness.
Should I explain what tedious work it is
putting role models together,
and how strategic pieces
sometimes get sucked up by this vacuum.
And while we intended to take
one giant leap for womankind,
I wound up taking one small step, alone.

What can I say at that moment
when our eyes meet in the mirror,
which they will.

What can I say to purple hair, black lips
and a nose ring?
What can I say?
Take care.

Hard Bargain
Cristin O'Keefe Aptowicz

I am auctioning off my virginity to the highest bidder.

And I am not,
and let me make this perfectly clear,
I am not being metaphorical here.

I want cold hard cash
for my tight hot
ethics.

I am sick of my virginity.

Back in the day, when we were eight, shit,
everyone was saving themselves for marriage,
or at least college, or at least a stable relationship
but now I've got friends little sisters giving
me advice on hand-jobs

And I don't have to put up with this crap
because I'm in college
and if there is one thing that I've learned
about virginity in college is that it is at best
an anecdote.

And not having an anecdote is one thing,
the reactions are a whole other story

All the girls with their,
"Well, don't worry.
You're bound to find someone."

S L A M

And all the guys with their, and sometimes these
are guys that I am interested in, all the guys with their
"Oh. Well, that explains a lot."

I don't need to be putting up with this shit

I am turning 20 in 149 days, and if there was
one thing that I have learned about virginity
anecdotes, it's that when you turn 20, the stories
go from charming and poignant
to depressing and pathetic.

So that's when it hit me:

Prostitution!

My plan, at first, was sell everything that I have of merit,
buy a roundtrip ticket to San Francisco, rent a car
and even though I don't drive, drive that car
down the darkest, poorest, scariest alley in San Fran,
the one that I read about in those Covenant House pamphlets
my mom would get from the Jehovah's Witnesses,
and I would find the youngest, most heroin-addicted,
wild-eyed, fresh-faced prostitute and open up
my car door and flash 200 crisp one dollar bills
and say, "Get in."

And I wouldn't tell him I'm a virgin.
I would tell him I'm a nympho, and I would take
him to a fancy hotel, and clean him up,
and lie him on silk sheets, and fuck him
like I've never fucked before, because
I haven't ever
fucked
before.

But then, just as this fantasy gets good, I remember:
Syphilis, gonorrhea, hepatitis A, B, C, the clap,
body lice, genital warts, crabs, scabies, chlamydia,
and AIDS.

And then it hits me.

Sell... myself... Fucking brilliant.

Fuck, I would be this thing,
this whole underground sex world thing.

Businessmen from Tokyo would
be calling businessmen in Wall Street,
who'd be calling up Heidi Fleiss in prison,
asking how can I get a piece of that?

Rich kids from L.A. would be logging in to
www.hymen.com for hourly updates.

Entire Italian villages would pool their money
so that I could lose it with the town schlong:
Ernesto, with the enormous cock that smells
suspiciously like flan and is crooked to the left.

I could sell the rights to HBO.

I would have to shave my pubic hair
into the Nike swoosh logo.

And after it was all over and the hype dies
down, I'll sit in my 36th floor apartment,
on my sofas made of twenties, and
I'd pull down the curtains, and turn
off the lights, and close my eyes,
and lie in the dark of room, and try
to remember what it was like to be

a virgin.

But until then,
let the bidding
begin.

Kissing With The Lights On
Daphne Gottlieb

you told me you like my mouth.
you want to kiss me.

my mouth is a wound and you
want to kiss me.

but you're like
that: you want to go
leaping over cliffs
you want to go
drinking poison
and then write pretty poems about it
and all i want to do is
fuck you.

you want flowers and sonnets and us
to be together until the end of the world and i'd
just like a blow job. i'd just like
to see your face when you come. i'd just like
to be friends.
that's what i'd really like.
something warm and snuggly like a friendship.
and to fuck you.

the flowers are going to die and the cliffs are
going to erode and we might as well go fuck
since we're going to anyway
we'll fuck and fight and eat and drink and smoke and fuck and
smoke and
fuck and
get married

and six months from now
we'll stop making the world stop
to fuck each other and

and one year from now

i'll get fat and you'll go bald and
i'll take prozac and you'll take viagra
i'll get obsessed with my biological clock
and my career
and you'll get obsessed with your hairline
and your career

and two years from now
you'd rather watch reruns than fuck me
and i'd rather be drinking than fuck you
so we'll drink in separate bars and one night
someone who likes my mouth will buy me a drink
that drink will be attached to a hand
there will be a human holding that drink
the kind with ears

and i will tell whoever it is
all about you
and how we used to forget to eat when we were in bed for three days
and your ears will be burning across town
where you are telling whoever it is how i don't understand you

and two years from now, that girl with that drink
she will nod that yes that i am nodding at you tonight
that nod, that yes that means you're not coming home
because just for a second the world has gone away
because just for a second there's someone who understands you

and that night it will be her pretty mouth you want
and that night i will pass out at home, alone
with a bottle that reminds me of us
because it'll be empty
because it'll be gone
i will pass out waiting for you
to come
home
listening to country music — and i hate
country music —
but i'll be feeling tragic
it'll be the most romantic moment

i've ever had and
i'll be alone

and you'll be across town
with that girl who right now is in high school
and right now i just met you
and right now i think you should take me home and fuck me
because it only gets uglier from here
we only get uglier from here
so take me to the edge of that cliff you love and
pour me a shot of your silky poison
you can take this mouth
this wound you want
but you can't kiss
and make it
better.

King on the Road
or Things to Do in Dallas When You're Drunk
Cass King

These are the things I learned when traveling: Thermal undies
are sometimes necessary, even in Santa Cruz. Laundry is grossly
undervalued in day-to-day society. Poets love to kiss. Poets love to
talk. Talk and kiss, kiss and talk. And drink. The best conversation
is always to be had in the smoking car. 200 carousing poets are not
welcome at the Heart O' Chicago Motor Inn. There are circuits
for touring poets that are evolving into what was once called a
"Vaudeville Wheel", a route that troupes would follow from town
to town. My family is much larger than I had assumed before I left
home.

Sure you want to tour? Things to ask yourself before you go:
Why am I doing this? Who are the lovers, pets and landlords that
might want to know where I am? What do I need? No, what do I
really need? Do I want to make money? How much? How? When
you have a grip on the above, make your intentions clear to the
universe at large, though it usually works better if you get specific,
like say… putting your query out in 250 words or less to everyone
you know and the Slam Listserv. Don't underestimate the value of

your telephone. Buy a map. Confirm minor details like money ahead of time. Get it down on paper. That way we can all be friends afterwards.

On Self-Promotion: Self-promotion, like masturbation, is a much-maligned reality that we all know is a lot of fun once you get into it. Go for it. Try to define what you do in a bio that makes people clamor to see you. Yes, you. For God's sake, don't believe your own press release. Even masturbation gets tiresome eventually. Feel free to change your self-definitions later, but GET SOME INFORMATION INTO THE HANDS OF YOUR HOSTS. Help them sell you. Give them expressive photos, intriguing poetry, press kits, anything that helps them interest the rest of the world in YOU. Get your photos scanned at a decent resolution and most of this can be done by email. Your Hotmail account is about to become your new best friend. Do it sooner than later. Good promotion happens 8 weeks ahead of time. (If you don't have a computer you can pay someone to scan and email your kit. It'll still cost you less than postage.)

Tech requirements: got any? Be clear. En Route: two words - Go Amtrak - cheap, bar car, roomy, bar car, lots of time to write in the bar car. (On a budget? Shhhhhh… bring your own bar.) Also, I've never met a born-again anything on an Amtrak train. I did meet a pro baseball player en route to California. I amused him by caring sweet fuck-all about sports. (My pangendered touring partner Ms. Spelt made up for me by performing his/her "Bigger than Baseball" poem for him late night in the lounge.) Needless to say, the service was excellent. (Don't drink the coffee.)

What to pack: a pen. Oh yeah, bring a towel, a pillow, a bedroll, books to read, books to sell, something that reminds you of home. Music. Maybe some clothes. Toiletries. Care and Feeding of your Hosts: you will be staying in people's homes. Definitely read *Sofa Surfing Handbook: A Guide for Modern Nomads* by Juliette Torrez. Love your hosts. Pack in what you pack out. Cook for them if you're in town long enough. Try to talk about something other than local slam politics. They will love you for it.

The Show: kick ass. But you knew that. Movin' the Merchandise: I have witnessed a few different methods of onstage promotion. In increasing degrees of effectiveness - The P.T. Barnum: sell your books like they are the last remaining shards of the Berlin Wall. The Sally Struthers: tell 'em that book sales mean gas and food money. The Out-Of-Town-Supastar-Slam-Dunk : (Also known as the Hunka-Hunka-Burnin' Verse) Just be so goddamn GOOD that you sell out of everything due to SHEER DEMAND. (This method takes considerable practice.)

Finally, I leave you with a scavenger hunt that all touring poets should undertake: The Palace of Fine Arts by moonlight (San Francisco), the Mütter Museum of Medical Oddities (Philadelphia, not for the squeamish), The Henry Miller Library (Big Sur), sautéed greens at Smoke Daddy's barbecue joint (next to Phyllis' Musical Inn, Chicago), the Columbia River Gorge at dawn by train, Shannon Falls (Squamish, B.C.). Enjoy your journey.

Untitled
Cass King

There is a kind of silence
That strengthens
As time lengthens
And Silence left unshattered is more golden than
That matter that the alchemists invented.

There is that silence where the I love you too bird
used to live.
I love you! I love you too...
I love you. I love you too.
I love you? I ...

There is a silence that lives
Finely sliced between venetian blinds
A silence that separates a stranger's cries
from the quickening glances
of safe, good people.
And as the rocks start to fly
a baby lies wailing on the quicksand sidewalk.
reached Mark Hi, you've Andrew, and the home of Paul...
call We can't take yours
you we can't take right now.
Call
Home of

If you're calling about what happened...
what happened
what happened
what happened?

Stop! Silence. Full stop.
After that gauntlet lies dropped
In the valley of the gutter
In the alley
By the window
Where the mother and the daughter were huddled
Who knew his last word would be _____
A summing up silence of violence interrupted.

Behind a dumpster
as three young men were
beating him, kicking him...
and then there were two, kicking, beating
and then there was one.
and the silent observation of two
was as deadly as the knife that slid into
My bleeding fresh/man of twenty one.

My air band Frank-n-furter,
high school principal kisser,
Unrequited lover
and forever, ever
anchor.

and now the Toronto Sun is blaring
"GOOD SAMARITAN" at me
and, staring out from the newspaper box
His eyes are forgiving
where mine are not.
I stick my
coins
into
the slot
and pick up
my copy of
Paul.

I will convince myself at his funeral
That we gather for his wedding
Expecting him to Lazarus down that aisle any minute,
to throw over that casket like Jesus
And tell the carrion cameras to go to obstetrics
And report someone new, for a change.

He throws me on his Kawasaki
And his family sings turn, turn, turn
We sacrifice maple leaves under our tires
And his family sings a time to every purpose under heaven
And I scream
I love you.....
I love you.....
I love you.....

And from somewhere from through these years
I hear that little bird return.
I love you too.

...Naming and Other Christian Things
Roger Bonair-Agard

At 31 I learn that Lena is short for Magdalene
  one of those enigmas of biblical lore
whore found religion
I have often questioned her motives – this love of Jesus Christ
this holy supplication to the son of Man

And I think about Lena my grandmother
  great big woman – skin of ashy obsidian
hair whitened by the burden of conviction
and I wonder about this business of weeping and foot washing;
    but I can only remember her iron hand and rigid schedules
  her admonition on catching me daydreaming on the outhouse roof
- Get down off that thing boy
- You have your book to study
- What kind of man do you intend to become?!
I recall her jacking up of my equally stern grandfather

reminding him of the folly
of any repeated attempts to hit her
    Never does Mary Magdalene come to mind
  not in the helpless 'weeping for the crucified' way
  not in the convenient Catholic depictions
of feminine frailty of morals and spirit
    I know of a Magdalene with fight
more Joan of Arc than Maid Marion
more Sojourner Truth than damsel in distress
  and I want to tell the withering two-dimensional ghost
couched and crumpled at the foot of the cross
      - Get up and fight woman!
      - Wake up and live if you love him!
      - Jack up the Pontius Pilate and refuse surrender

at 4 I was beaten for disrespect of my grandfather
at 8, because I was satisfied with only a 75 in Math -
because she knew   having fought battles based purely on
conviction
that she was preparing a man for the holiest of crucifixions
    there would be no washing of feet here
    no flimsy eruption of tears
only the austerity of a warrior
and a Puritan insistence on perfection and effort
  the creases through her aged jowls softening
only when she thought I needed to eat   to get strong
     -Son yuh lookin thin; come and get some food

a name orients one to his universe the Lakotas believed
a change in name meant a chance for improvement
for the child who was not doing well
    so having learned the root of my grandmother's name
I cannot summon the sympathy for Mary Magdalene
  cannot help her weep tears of distress
only wish I could retroactivate a name change for her
show her my grandmother carrying 30 lb sacks of coffee
  dragging her swollen leg behind her
rising from her deathbed to fight her daughter's battles

One day if I am worthy of her expectations

I will become a man worth crucifying
and all her beatings
her lessons
her Puritanism and super-human strength
will have taught me
that surrender is not an option

On that day I expect to see
standing at the foot of whatever urban cross they fashion
all five-foot-ten of Lena
pointing one huge gnarled finger at me
   the shining authority of her eyes
coming from the black forest of her flesh
the white electricity of her hair
lips trembling in rage
        - Get down off that thing boy and fight!!
        - What kind of man do you expect to become?!

My Million Fathers, Still Here Past
Patricia Smith

Hallelujah for grizzled lip, snuff chew, bended slow walk and shit
talkin'.
Praise fatback, pork gravy, orange butter, alaga syrup, grits,
and egg sammiches mashed 'tween sheets of wax paper,
you are three-day checker games and white whiskey sucked
through holes where teeth was. All glory to the church deacons,
nappy knobs of gray hair greased flat and close to conk,
cracked voices teetering and testifying, bless you postmen,
whip cloth shoe shiners, the porters bowing low and sweet,
I hear all of you swear-scowling, gold-tooth giggling over games
of bid whist and craps, your thin shaky voices pushing away
the promises of the promised land and in your upright lift,
my sad fathers, I see you young again, your shining eyes,
you spitshined and polished on sluggish Greyhound coaches
or colored in colored car of a silver train from Pine Bluff, Ark.,
from Aliceville, Ala., Oscaloosa, Minneola, Greenwood,
Muscle Shoals, heading for the north where factories were sex,
sleek and churning like a woman, north, which felt like an ice cube

dragged slowly over your burning skin. You mail order zoot suit wide wing felt hats to dip low over one eye, you learn pimp walkin', dip, swivel click heel tap and you kickin' up hot foot to get down one time, acrylic slow drag and blues through to bone and bony hip bump when the jukebox teases and praise to the eagle what flies on Friday and the Lincoln Mark, the Riviera, the Electra Deuce and a Quarter, the always too much car for what you were. You are the lucky number, the dream book, here is to your mojo, your magic real, roots and conjures and long-dead plants in cotton pouches, the if yo foot get swept spit on the broom superstition, griots of rickety back porch and city sidewalk, and you, my million fathers, still here past chalk outlines, dripping needles and prison cots, past whuppings, tree hangings and the call of war, past JB stupor and drive-bys, you are survivor, scarred and running, choking back news of thyroid, your high pressure, dimming eyes, your weather hurtin' leg, here's for the secret of your rotting teeth, the tender bump on your balls, your misaligned back, the wild corn on your little toe, the many rebellions of your black and tired body. I watch you now, all of my fathers, clucking forgotten lust past your gums, squeezing runny eyes shut to conjure the dreamy outline of a woman. I will rub your weary head, dance close to you, shuck you silver peas for dinner.

He is Otis, my father, but you are Willie Earl and James and Ernest and Jimmy Lee, you are all my fathers as if he was not stopped by a blues wailing bullet and you are all his smoky voice unreeling into my pen, all of you old black men, gentle Delta, I grieve you wandering toward death, I celebrate you clinging to life. Open your bony dark-veined arms and receive me, your daughter, who is taking on your last days as her very blood, who is learning your whispered language too late to stop your dying, but not too late to tell

this story.

Eulogy of Jimi Christ
Reggie Gibson

I.
"look at the sky
turn a hell fire red lawd

S L A M

somebody's house is burnin down down down

look at the sky turn a hell fire red lawd
somebody's house is burnin down down down down..."

burn it down

burn it down

you burned it all the way down Jimi

made us burn
in the flame
that became yo sound Jimi

grabbin ol legba
by his neck
made him
show you some respect

hoochie man
coochie man
stranglin him
hoochie coochie hoodoo man
wranglin him voodoo chile

made
his
steel
strings sing
ache
bend
break

sin
capitulate
and give in
to the will
of yo beautifully blessed fingers
bewitchingly

bleeding
bittersweet

south paw
serendipitous
sighs

and strained
stratocaster tears

soothin burnin
twistin turnin
into steam
as they fell
and careened
toward all hellbound souls

only to
roll
back into yo
gypsied eyes

to fornicate
copulate
be sodomized
by penetration beautiful
of sweatband born acid rain

II.
a purple haze running through
you brain drained into the veins
of daytrippers turned acid angel
by yo gift of little wings

who with the aid
of yo mary cryin winds soared
not merely above
around and through
crosstown traffic
along and well beyond

S L A M

watchtowers to realm
where gods made love
to little miss strange
foxy ladies in little red houses
over yonder

and on rainy days
would sit back
shoot craps
with laughing sam's dice
while boastin bout who had
the most experience

III.
how the musebruise
of yo sadomasochistic bluesoozed
through floors and l.s.d. doors

leavin psychedelic relics wrecked
on phosphorescent shores

talkin bout that night
you got right
at yo height
rocked woodstock
played yo remade
american anthem
that had all the flowers
in the garden chanting

"go head brotha
piss off the power
structure brotha"

"say fuck ya to the
structure brotha
one mo time one last time
befo it's you last time brotha"

stick and move

hit and run
stick and move
hit and run

try to get
you ass beyond
the grip of the grim one

try to get
yo ass out of
the sight line of death

try to get
you ass past
the reach of
the reaper
by dodging
that son of a bitch
betwixt the expanse
of jangled cacophonous clouds
and hiding out in shadows
flooded with feedback

jimi   the anointed

jimi   the christ

manically depressed
maniacally dressed
manifested messiah

impaled upon the neck
of that thang you loved the best

yo one hears hearts true burning desire

jimi christ

forever walkin
on the waters

S L A M

of a bad trip

turnin all of
them bad trips
into wine

castin yo net
upon the waters
of a bad trip
just to see what's there
for you to find

jimi christ

patron saint
of divine distortion

too soon
did you force
the hand of demise

but i ain't pissed
at you gypsy eyes

cause right now
we diggin on the thought
of you and you homeboy god

being somewhere
out there in electric ladyland
sippin celestial moonshine

bout to tune axes
cut heads
and go
toe to toe
blow for blow
lick for lick
and stick for stick
but ha!!!

first you and god
gotta stop and laugh
yo asses off/at that
fat assed
slurred mouth
country fuck
over there in the corner

dig him wearin that rhinestone
studded jacket
and jacked up
bell bottoms

trying to sing lead
at the same time he twists his torso
in an attempt to molest an innocent sheep

jimi christ
too soon did you force
the hand of demise
but i can't be too pissed
at you gypsy eyes

cause i dig that any mother lover
who lived a life like you led
deserved to die any death desired

to die youngto die
highto die stonedto
die freeto die youngto die high

to die stonedto die
freeeeeeeeeeeeeeeeeeee

all we wanted was one time
just   one   time

to stand next to yo fire

Canis Rufus (Ode to Chaka Khan)
Dana Bryant

electric lady
knifin' the curtain
open with bejeweled fingers

her head
laden with citrus sweetened hairs—
medusian ropes swingin' hot embers
hennaed bells—
her lips
plentiful soft
and smackin'
sweet badass's
TELL ME SOMETHIN' GOOD
her stomach
stripped of all
but bronze blue flesh—
beaded rings of baby peacock feathers—
her hips
swayin' chains
of lilies laced wid sense-amelia—
MARRY DOOJAH WANNA FUNK WID ME?
her crotch
explodin' light—
mound of venus rainin' salt n flame
on
open lifted stadium faces

she bodacious
she be
    jungle bunny   bessie smith   demoness
    howlin' at the moon
she be
    the voodoo chile jimi hendrix plucked
    strings to conjure up
she be
    the brass ring my mama said
    good colored girls must not reach for

she be
    the circe
    that esoteric nut deigned
    to tell me was too much

she too literal
she too extreme
much too seamy
much too obscene

i say

SCREAM SISTA

your ward 8
sensibility
speaks for me
praise the day
i first heard
your illicit moans
ring stereo
in smoke filled
blue lit
basements

when my daddy said
SHE can't be music
give charlie mingus some play
make room for charlie mingus
ring in the new year wid...
nat king cole?

say?
can't be music?
if she
rushes in deep
my well
like poetry
like flush
like semen

like spit
like your bloodied face
reboundin' one mo time
off the blows
of a so-called
black-faced bimbo
broke down
from wailin'

                nu blues

broke down
from wailin'

                nu news

broke down
from wailin' out
beyond image
to me
can't be music?

Et Cetera and All That Jazz
Ariana Waynes

a beer. it started with a beer. in a bar. i bought for you, you
bought for me, i picked you up with, was picked up with a beer.
had i ever been so bold? to ask to say yes to make eye contact to
hold an offered gaze? was i so lonely brazen drunk trusting horny
rich to think that someone like you could be bought with a
beer... so poor that a beer was all it took? nickels into a jukebox,
a maybe in your eyes, in mine, a hand offered smaller than i'd
expected. false starts and leading, being led across the 4 by 6 foot
excuse for an almost maybe dance floor. my toes were crushed
beneath your accidental step i apologized for tromping on your
foot we fumbled, it was all over, it was a bad idea, it was not. the
truck driving types pointedly ignoring us who cared that the
races weren't right, that the faces didn't quite mesh that we
could be lynched the moment we stepped out the door... we
stepped out of the door. you held it for me, i opened it for you
and stood there, my fingers shivering on the metal. i'd never
done this quite before. you said it might be fun. the car the truck

the key in the ignition the hair twirling around the finger the nervous closeness the broken heater the jokes hanging out the window, my fingers on the steering wheel, my hands fixing the rearview mirror while you drove. don't look back. don't look back. the jokes the infinite maybes and finite what-ifs with finite solutions and consequences and weren't we supposed to be adults and whatever happened to all those responsibilities like jobs and families and cats and parakeets and sons and nieces and nosy aunts and boyfriends and wives and something called sunday dinner forgotten because of some tight fabric stretched across delicate oversized shoulders beneath a round square face that held eyes nearly as thirsty as mine. and maybe that was a first. and maybe you were like water but you didn't know it. and maybe you were like fire and i just couldn't see it. and maybe we wouldn't get burned. and maybe we would. maybe we'd be each other's end. maybe we'd die tomorrow tonight. maybe we already did. and this was punishment for our sins. and this was heaven. and maybe i wouldn't be able to endure this car ride, my foot testing the gas at red light after another, awkwardness hanging in the air between us like a child in the middle seat, antsy, bobbing up and down, are we there yet, are we there yet? and maybe i'd explode with waiting in a foreign passenger seat for the traffic ticket that surely would come with driving 90 miles an hour or so to a place i'd never been before, to my home, and the cop would pull us over, the light glaring in my eyes like his distaste, all right miss, son, madam, sir, can you show me please your license, registration, et cetera and all that jazz, please step out of the car, you two shouldn't be together filthy perverts you think you can get away with that abominable disgusting, not under my jurisdiction you won't my hands hugging the oh shit bar, fiddling with the stereo, sliding over just a little bit closer to you for warmth or something resembling something else that my mind couldn't quite put syllables to. and then we were there. here. my home. some place i'd never seen before and couldn't quite stomach. a dilapidated quaint enormous freshly-painted falling apart mansion shack apartment townhouse ranch whatever in the front door and off the clothing forgotten in heaps on the floor couch furniture. i hold am held by you, flesh tumbling into flesh clinging onto flesh rubbed raw and worn and tired and alive and wet, hairs rising, goose bumps growing contagiously. We move together, one creature dancing, an octopus swimming through slightly coffee-stained air, smudging the boundaries between our bodies piled heavily on the hardwood floor because our hunger couldn't make it to a mattress. almost obscenely you take me into your mouth and we swell together, i vulnerable beneath your breath, quivering like the day i was born, ecstatic, on fire. i take allow myself to be taken by you fuck you am fucked penetrate am raped violate acquiesce. and i can't remember who was on top and i can't remember who thrust what into whom and i can't remember who got the latex and lube and how they were used and on whom by whom i can't remember what diseases weren't transmitted i can't remember what clothing who wore and i can't remember why the faces didn't quite mesh i just remember lust equaling love for just a moment and all the rest dripping away into puddles on the floor that we'd clean up in the morning when we really saw one another for the first time as anything other than me and you. i remember thinking i could die before then. laughing.

The Horse Cock Manifesto
Beau Sia

there's a rumor going around
that asian men
are hung like horses!

i don't know who would think to say such things,
who would want to say such things,
who would sit around and say,
"what can i do now
to tarnish the names of asians everywhere?"
blurting out the obvious
in such a crude manner.

but some menace, villain, nemesis, enemy, threat
to the asian community as i know it,
has been spreading around that

"asian men are hung like horses!"
and i hate the idea of the fact,
as the word has spread farther than i can control.
my lies seem to be of no use
as i am continually disproved,
and i cannot stop them,
a flood of people swarming into asia,
fucking around the clock with asian men!

there are women in sweden
who are crying over their blonde-haired,
disastrously blue-eyed beau's minuscule proportions.

there are teenage girls in africa, disgusted
at the lack of feeling
between legs
when warrior men give them their best.

there are southern belles gasping for something more
than the triteness
of redneck penetration.

and this has ruined the ecological, sociological, sexological
breeding patterns of the whole world,
as some nitwit has let out that

"asian men are hung like horses!"

i don't know why these things happen,
as someone had to reveal that we are great with laundry
and convenience stores,
and someone else let loose how we all know martial arts,
and just recently i found out that everyone knows how
    goddamned good at math
we are,

but now
i face the most humiliating release of our culture,
as the woman who has sworn vendetta on us has claimed that

"asian men are hung like horses."
it ends up that i can't take this anymore.
i can't live like this anymore,
with sex five times a day,
sex eighteen hours a day,
sex everyday,
sex in every fashion known to man this side of the kama sutra,
all because there is some one woman organization dedicated
to spreading the rumor that

"asian men are hung like horses!"

and i don't want to hear it,
because the pager is beeping off the hook,
cell phone won't stop ringing,
email box full,
and the anonymous notes i keep finding
in my coat pockets are getting to be more
than these literary eyes can stand,

and it is always so uncaring,
as it is name, number, place, time.

no list of hobbies, interests, or favorite colors.

and this is the marked men that we asians have become
as the demand increases and we decrease,
no longer able to take the abuse,
phalli rubbed too raw for description.

and now we face the sword proudly
as we do not like it to be known,
that thing,
that horrid thing,
that thing some vindictive whore
must have said at a really big party,
very loudly,

"asian men are hung like horses!"

i don't know how to act around people anymore,
as eyes remain fixated
on my crotch,
and i now fear the day that someone
starts spreading the rumor that

"asian men have narrow eyes!"

because i don't know how we'll go around unnoticed again.

Deconstructing the Prop Slam,
or Anatomy of a Prop
Lisa Martinovic

The Rule
No props. Generally, poets are allowed to use their given environment and the accoutrements it offers — microphones, mic stands, the stage itself, chairs on stage, a table or bar top, the aisle — as long as these accoutrements are available to other competitors as well. The rule concerning props is not intended to squelch the spontaneity, unpredictability, or on-the-fly choreography that people love about the slam; it's intent is to keep the focus on the words rather than objects.

The Definition
Prop: an object or article of clothing introduced into a performance with the effect of enhancing, illustrating, underscoring, or otherwise augmenting the words of the poem.

Make no mistake, friends, the National Poetry Slam is very serious business. And strict! There are scores and decimal points, official spiels and protest committees, rules and penalties, and tumultuous, bloodletting, nitpicking meetings where sleep-deprived, hungover poets debate whether or not rules were broken intentionally or even broken at all. It's all very confusing, and dreadfully stressful. Mercifully, every year the National Poetry Slam organizers in their wisdom provide all manner of outlets to relieve the collective tension that is slam. There are steamy, panty-soaking erotica readings, head-to-head haiku combat matches, shit-slinging all-scatology open mics, and my favorite: The Prop Slam.

As you know by now, if you've been paying attention at all, most slams, and certainly the official National Poetry Slam competition, all are adamant about one thing: NO PROPS. The classic slam is the very model of simplicity. In it the poet is allowed her words, her voice, and whatever she can do with her body (but, importantly, not her clothes) for three achingly short — or torturously long — minutes. But performance poets are such a creative bunch, sometimes we just want MORE. The word alone is not enough to convey the fullness of our vision, the profundity of our message. We want to enter to the sound of Harleys throttling, or flaunt our full cabaret-chanteuse selves. And we want to improv our way to a win with a Beat-flavored cancione about imperialist swine, accompanied by beers'n'bongos. We don't want our imaginations fettered by no stinking rules! We want to go completely WILD. And for slammers thus bent — praise Jesus! — we have the prop slam.

That having been said, I don't think prop slams are for everyone. Many slammers choose, for obscure reasons known only to themselves, to remain traditionalists. But if a prop slam is in you, baby, you can feel it rumbling from deep in your soul or your gut or some other organ that best remains nameless. The inspiration for your maiden effort may come as a complete surprise. One day you're jogging or taking a nap and you're thinking about a new poem or an old poem in a new way, and you get this idea, this silly idea, and suddenly you're giggling and thinking maybe — oh, god, I couldn't do that... could I?

But once the seed has sprouted, there is no stopping it. Over the next few weeks the idea grows and grows until, like Jack's mutant beanstalk, it is out of all proportion and control. Before you know it, you're prowling hobby stores for plastic fish or dolls' wigs, pouring over exotic fabrics that just scream San Francisco Castro District, sawing and hammering, sewing and gluing merrily away in your basement. Friends and loved ones worry, start to ask questions. Pay attention now, folks, here's your first tip from a veteran prop slammer: keep your prop plan a secret! The element of surprise is crucial to a successful prop performance. Go deep cover. Don't tell ANYONE who doesn't have the need to know. Only people who are part of your performance should know just exactly how you plan to embarrass them. And sometimes even that's not the case.

I will often choose an unwitting subject from the audience to serve as my prop a few scant moments before I'm set to perform. This keeps everyone on their toes and often provides a great humanitarian service to audience members challenged to go where they've never gone before. For example, at the '99 Chicago Nationals, one poet didn't know if she could master the role I asked of her ("perverted flamenco dancer" to my Large Tattooed Penis). But I had confidence. I urged her on and lo, when it came time to clench that fake long stemmed rose between her teeth, she stole the scene with a flourish.

But first, let's talk shop. Prop slam pieces tend to be either sexy or funny — and if your piece is both, get ready to rock the house. You are allowed to use costumes, musical instruments, animals, other people — pretty much anything your fertile poet's mind can conjure. Prop poems can get quite elaborate, so I encourage you to allow yourself lots of rehearsal time. As with any other type of slam, there's little more exasperating than getting the highest raw score but losing due to overtime deductions. (I speak from my own tragic experiences here.) Mercifully, you will be allowed to set up your equipment on-stage before the clock starts ticking. More than one MC has chastened the audience "Now, don't try this at home, folks" as I scrambled like a dramaturge possessed, furiously assembling chairs, curtains, and an array of costumes to rival the most lavish drag queen revue. So go ahead and make the most of that time to get all your props in a row. The audience will be intrigued (to a point — don't push it.) Then, unleash your madness!

Perhaps an account of one Prop's evolution would be helpful for those readers who may yet be wondering "Is the Prop Slam really for me?" I've got this poem, 'If I Were A Man, I'd Have A Big Dick'. It's always been great fun to perform and even audiences in the Biblically Belted community where I lived generally found it entertaining, if vaguely scandalous. When our local scene scheduled its first Prop Slam, it seemed a natural. Given my environment it was no surprise that the idea itself came to me as a religious vision — there, next to the Virgin Mary, there shimmered a long purple tube sock, while in the background a celestial choir chimed Thrust Me, Thrust Me into your arms, O Lordy. I came to in a cold sweat. Of course, the old High Holy Purple Tube Sock

SLAM

gambit! Immediately, I set about constructing this neo-religious icon. I shopped Wal-Mart for the very finest in sox. Under cover of night, I dyed the one sacrificial sock a plummy yet eye-catching purple, stirring and chanting incantations (having reverted to Pagan during this transmutation process) over an old wood stove. Next I inserted my fingers into a warm ooze that I haven't felt in decades. Equipped with only flour, water and strips of newspaper, and a kindergartner's sense of delight, I fashioned a startling rendition of a penile glans with the humble art form that is papier mache. I painted the head a complimentary shade of purple and affixed it to the toe of the sock to form a very long, flexible sheath into which a cohort of my choosing could slip his or her arm, thrust and romp, thus creating the simulacrum of an exceptionally healthy male organ. And since he was so immense and hailed from Arkansas, I called him Buck.

My initial vision (the one from the Virgin Mary) was to have Buck appear, as if by magic, from between my legs, during the performance. Nothing more. But the budding turbo-prop slammer in me, once liberated, would not rest. Many's the night I lay abed tossing and turning, unable to sleep as ideas burned like thousand-watt bulbs in my prop-charged brain. I envisioned Buck on stage with me, all naked and undignified, and, sharing his shame, I wept. Through my tears I meditated on the text of my poem: "… a regal and handsome dick…" But of course, he needs a crown! Which I proceeded to craft from cardboard and gold foil. Next came "a riding the range… kind of dick" Yup, a l'il black felt cowboy hat was the answer, and I found one just his size at the local Hobby Lobby! And so it went as I continued to take the art form to its logical extension: my prop had props!

Now, I'm a stickler for accuracy in costuming so it was important that each of Buck's head ornaments be secured around his umm… chin… with an elastic band lest they slip off in the vigor of performance and spoil the delicate illusion of verisimilitude I'd worked so hard to create. Similarly, I prepared a Spanky-style curtain from an old sheet, and would have to enlist two more confederates at the slam willing to hold it on-stage between me and the power behind my prop. All I needed now was someone to play Buck. Obviously, this is a meaty consideration for prop slammers who are relying on others to play a significant role in their poem. And for my part, I didn't want just anyone playing my fantasy organ. My roommate at the time was Chuck, an affable Army drill sergeant and combat vet who was just plain honored when I asked him to play Buck. We spent many hours of merriment rehearsing and dress rehearsing right up until the big night. Since I hadn't told a soul about my plans, Buck's debut was a delicious surprise and truly he, with Chuck at the groin, brought down the house. Chuck turned out to be quite adept at conveying the nuanced role I'd written for Buck (see my earlier observation about giving others the opportunity to shine as a part of your performance). We won handily. And in this pre-Nationals trial run we learned some important lessons, not the least of which is that Buck needed his own personal dresser. As you can well imagine, it was simply too much for Chuck to remember his cues, change costumes with his left hand only, and make a papier mache penis emote convincingly all at once! So, in Austin at the '98 Nationals, I marshaled all my resources. My teammate, Brenda Moossy, served as dresser, while our coach, Eve Stern, played Buck. Rehearsing in the hotel room was one of the highlights of that National Slam for me.

That afternoon, the Prop Slam was SRO. My name was drawn near the beginning of the show. Tension mounted as the audience watched the curtain go into place, hiding the mystique of Buck like a latter day Wizard of Oz. His grand entrance was greeted with a deafening cheer and the entire performance was a nonstop laugh-fest from crotch to crown. The crowd ate us up like great oral sex. I'd be remiss if I didn't acknowledge that much of the credit is due to Eve's skill as a thespian and her intuitive grasp of the male organ's psyche. Her portrayal of Buck in all his manifestations was nothing short of a tour de force. We finished to a standing ovation and in that moment my life was complete. I'd accomplished what I was sent here to do in this incarnation. I share my story now in hopes that some among you will avail yourselves of the tremendous opportunity for spiritual growth that is the Prop Slam, and reap its rich rewards. Now go out there and have a ball... or a penis... or a python... or...

If I Were A Man, I'd Have A Big Dick
Lisa Martinovic
[annotated for prop slam]

You know
if I were a man
I'd have a big dick   [enter B., with enthusiasm]
I mean a real handful
not freak show or anything
but a tool with some heft to it
I'd have the kind of dick
that inspires covert double takes   [B. peeks stage left]
in public urinals
Yes, mine would be an impressive organ
I'd have to mail order condoms   [L. rolls plastic bag onto B.]
to insure a fit that didn't impede my circulation
Small women might feel a slight clutch of fear   [B. recoils]
at first sight but
I'd be gentle   [B. strokes thigh]

Mine would be a regal and handsome dick
                    [B. enters wearing crown]
dangling or erect, it would be perfectly plumb
not bent or veering off at some peculiar angle   [B. bends]
as if trying escape its god given role in life   [B. withdraws swiftly]
It would hang like a masterpiece in the Louvre
                [B. emerges with portrait around neck]
a veritable cock of the gods
Zeus or Thor would be proud to sport this rocket
                    [B. zooms upwards]
while a mortal man bearing such a dick
walks thorough the world with a
cock-sureness that other men can only envy   [L. grabs B.]

No one would ever be fool enough to call Big John here a
weenie   [B. shakes head]
At rest he is a meaty sausage
all latent power
perpetually poised to spring into action   [B. becomes erect]
at the merest whisper of provocation   [L. strokes B.]

Once engaged, some caution must be exercised
                            [B. thrusts vigorously toward audience]
If, in my zeal, I slip out and miss on reentry
                            [B. shakes head downwards]
well, I'm in deep shit
So how do I know I'd have a big dick?
Because I'm an American, damnit!
                            [B. emerges in black cowboy hat]
Male or female, I was born macho
outfitted with a certain confidence
a swagger even
an attitude
that befits a man with a well hung slab o ham
I said I'm an American!
It's my birthright
I'm entitled to look down and gaze upon
the finest lovebone this side of Homo Erectus
                            [B. swivels slowly, looks up at L.]
That's right, I damn well deserve
the endowment of a quintessential American dick
a strong, silent
riding the range   [B. simulates gallop]
slide into town, take no prisoners and slide on out   [B. exits]
kind of dick
A Colt 45 shotgun M-16 howitzer MX missile of a dick
                            [B. enters encased in projectile weapon]
A grunting, thrusting, strutting, rutting creature
                            [B. makes repeated jabs]
that's built to take the heat and do some damage
                            [B. launches missile into audience; exits]
I'm talking about a dick that means business
                            [B. enters with red necktie and attitude]
a laissez faire, world's policeman, corporate takeover
                            [L. and B. make sweeping circular motions]
in the guise of a one-eyed fleshy barbarian   [B. exits]
My fellow Americans
our national dick is on a mission from god!
                            [B. emerges in angel costume]
World domination
one inch at a time   [B. strokes deep]

Who could resist such a rousing destiny?   [B. exits]
No contest, baby
If I was a man
I'd have me a
big ole
American
dick   [B. emerges with American flag protruding from urethra]

Big Rig
Krystal Ashe

My man's gotta Big Rig
really, he has a Big Rig.
not an RV - 4x4 - flatbed - pick em up truck or double wide duelly.
He has an 18-wheeler that he drives around Chicago
like a four banger, straight six or V8.

When I first saw him climb down that cab,
I knew I had to haul some ass with him.
Besides his Armani suit
his Kenneth Cole loafers
and his Mary Tyler Moore hairdo,
I knew right from the start that he wasn't your average truck
driver.
I could tell he was a man of taste.
His cab was absent of those flaming eagle sunset murals,
and silhouettes of naked ladies didn't ride *his* mud flaps.
I could also tell he was a man of mystery
his name wasn't painted on the driver's door

So one night I spied his truck was parked in front of the Green Mill,
he was alone at the bar, chocolate martini in hand,
swingin' his hair and snappin' his fingers to The Mighty Blue Kings,
I knew this was my chance to get some breaker 69.
I went right on up and asked,
"What's your handle and can you handle me?"
He took a drag off his Dunhill and said, "Roger."
"So, Roger, do you make home deliveries?"
he said,

"What do you want me to haul?"
I said,
"How bout some ass?"
He gave me a once over and said,
"10-4, good buddy! That sounds like a hand job."
I said, "Roger, Roger. I acknowledge."
I thought my neighbors hated me when I came home on my ex's
    Harley,
ever heard an 18-wheeler go down a residential street at 5 a.m.?
One neighbor thought it was the millennium hitting Chicago,
but let me *tell* you,
the way he maneuvered that big ol' truck of his
down my narrow street,
well...

My friend Irene told me she felt sorry for me,
I asked why,
"Well, come on," she said,
"Talk about dick extension vehicles... Your guy drives a sixty
    foot penis!"
Now, I told her *nothing*, but let me tell you,
my baby knows all those gears, and at 22,
he can shift me through all 18 every night.
He doesn't need that 100 mile coffee
and he's no lead-foot or Roger ramjet either.

Now, dating a guy with a semi has its perks.
If we're on the move to an eat um up joint
like Mia Francesca, Scoozi or Gejas,
and we find ourselves in the mood
we got that bed right there in the cab!
We can pull right over and get horizontal!
I know what you're thinking
"Parking has got to be a hassle,"
and believe me, we don't wanna feed the bears,
we're always on the lookout for Kojack with a Kodak,
but parking Roger's semi,
is actually easier and cheaper than parking a Yugo.
He pulls into the no parking zones,
who is gonna tow an 18-wheeler?

And we *never* pay for valet.
When we pull up to Spy Bar or Trendy Club for a quick drink
we toss the keys to the valet and we always
find them standing in a circle when we come back out
still looking for someone who can "drive that big thing."

And talk about convoys, if we still wanna socialize
at 4 a.m. when Martini Ranch kicks us out,
we can bring fifty of our closest friends to the after hours!
And if the party gets busted,
we got 200 sq. ft. to throw down in!!!
Oh, don't worry about Roger being a Willy Weaver,
he only drinks Evian after midnight.
Well, gotta put the pedal to the metal,
Roger just pulled up, it's time for a quickie.
'Til I see you next,
Keep your nose between the ditches and Smokey out of your britches.

Fingertips & Laughter
Nisa Ahmad

where iguanas bathe in moonlight
while bats dance to mariachi bands
his smile haunts me
like stealing peaks at the pool boy pablito
as he gazes into avocado trees
he teases me
with back shots of his frontals
as he leaves arches like angels' tears
against the day
and he knows i'm watching
yet only cracks me a smile
from behind
my friend
reminds me of mercados
where chickens are pollos
and still have feathers and heads
as he spreads his fingertips
around my hips

palming me like holding coconuts
and his laughter sings
salty sweet
like margaritas in husks
on beaches at dusk
stealing kisses like time
we become
pancakes of chocolate
connected by stars twinkling
and school girls rushing home
i am
racing into the fingertips of his laughter
bathing in the light of his eyes
hoping he will feed me
stealing kisses like time
holding me like palming coconuts
not so gently against the indigo velvet of night
and in mornings i finger his prints
like tarot cards or beach glass
breathing into the space we once filled
watching a steady flow of emotions rise
sending thoughts hurling
like pebbles across mountain streams
headed home to sea
and he reminds me of indians
weaving bags of yarn and leather
wordlessly disappearing back into the mountains
palming me
with his eyes
and my breasts giggle
as my hips writhe
between his fingertips
eyes following
the hollow and swell of his pelvis
pounding like waves crashing sand
like hands pounding congas
and our thighs meet
where the horizon of his abdomen
drops off into the fertile valley of his manhood
as my chin seeks

the delta of his collar bone
trafficking shooting stars
into the handmade altar of my heart
beating
like sole of boys
rushing to the panderia
before closing
i am
racing into the fingertips of his laughter
washing over us
like moon beams
i am

The Emperor's Second Wife
Adrienne Su

I light the extra room and stay there nights
when I'm not called. I curl in the empty quilt
and know she's with him. I pull the blankets tight

and hope I won't remember how she goes
to him in nothing, original and dank, denying
little. She understands his need; she knows

I'm filling in the nights when she's unwilling.
She knows I'm twelve years old and only starting.
But I'm the one whose sleep is shallow, spilling

into day. He's everything to me but lover.
He tells me, if we don't make love, it's right.
It's best my spirit stay intact, all over.

No one else must know. They think the two
of us are fucking all the time we're here.
But we just talk. The rustling girls who do

my nails are scared for me. They think I'll swell
before the winter. But in the chamber's privacy
he only wants to hold me, kiss me, touch, and tell

me I am gracious. He won't do violation
— that's how he calls it — so we lie beside
each other, tumid with desire and the patience

of two statues. *It's wrong*, he says. *You're young.*
You should be learning grammar. I cover my face
when he says these things. I ache. I've just begun

to see the error. He thinks girls happen slower,
that as long as we're unopened, we're immune
to breaking. He imagines I'm intact all over.

That lady must go. When I learn magic,
I'll erase her, have her put away for stealing.
But she doesn't hate me back. She brings elastic

ribbons, ties my hair in twists. She comes
with plates and pastries. She gives me stockings,
pins, and slips, and asks me if our husband's won

me over. I tell her he is all a girl
could want, and more. She snickers when I say it,
then agrees. In recent months our emperor's revealed

another side. He can't be still. She likes
my work. It's clear she thinks I do the service.
We talk about his mouth, his hands, his eyes

and feet. She says, when I'm a few years older
I'll be deadly. She thinks I never cry,
that I'm serene, divine, immune. Intact, all over.

Tree
Edwin Torres

And these hands
uprooted — 3 fingers splintered
And these scragged needles

ripped through earth
And this field
captured by violet sound
And this tree
how was it placed to be looked at
And now midnight
And this parade has passed
And that star field
And these fingernails
eleven stars in every cuticle
And this grip
this sky molten solstice
And all these earth dreamers
wrapped around us
And all the long shadows
like me...
Placed to be looked at
far from home

In A Place Where
Patricia A. Johnson

crepe myrtle hangs
brushes the ground
japanese beetles
ride each other's back
the leaf eaten away beneath them
hills and mountains
carve out the sky
random pieces in a rag quilt
queen anne's lace, ragweed
sweetpeas and joe-pye weed
choke the roadside
there are no signs stating:
wildflowers, do not pick

in a place where
crows big as cats
feed in fields dotted

with wagon-wheel hay bales
cattle, flies sipping
from their eyes
seek shade from trees
along the fence line
in a place where
you drink a breath and
hay, manure, magnolia
clover and wild primroses
ride the intake of air

a dirt road is swallowed by pines
smoke rises above silver maples
the smell of hog killing
hangs in the air
heavy shoes crunch gravel
down and up an incline
to the trailer
offset by trash
circled by weeds

on a mattress
in the front yard
crumpled and headless
a Black man burns
July 25, 1997; G.P. Johnson
was burned alive and decapitated
in rural Grayson County, Virginia
in a place where
I call home.

Albuquerque
Juliette Torrez

as i drive down albuquerque streets
edges of houses pop out of gray sky
undisguised by barren trees
twenty-three shades of brown
stucco painted to look like adobe

we're driving past, past the porches
where strings of red chile
hang there in welcome
how now brown town?
and it's good to be here
though when i'm gone
i don't miss you much
i even dogged you, albuquerque
because you are
a hard hearted town
dressed in fake mud
being something you're not
personality split by two sides of the city
uptown and downtown, the heights and the valley
split by businessmen
developing their property
you never had a good image of yourself,
albuquerque
you don't love yourself the way
san francisco loves itself
the way seattle loves itself
the way santa fe loves itself
and i wonder what crime
stained these hills
that made you such a hard hearted town
dressed in brown
ribboned in interstate asphalt
and a poisoned river
i'm fascinated by your sinister side,
albuquerque
and pray you don't claim me
as a blood sacrifice
but when i come back
i see the way the sunset hits the sandias
and remember what it was
that i miss about this town
i see the morning light bright blue
the smell of cedar burning in the air
and remember what i miss
about this town

and when i go to the frontier restaurant
and ask for a green chile burger
they know exactly what it is
and they give it to me
and i remember what i miss
about this town
albuquerque
i love you i hate you
i'll always come back to you
the land of entrapment
a curse or a blessing
i don't know the answer
i just keep returning

Understand
Kenn Rodriguez

When I ask A.P.D. what they need
helicopters with spotlights for
When I ask Don't you know
that if you treat people like animals
that they usually react like animals?
The mailman brings me
a three hundred word letter on crisp, pristine
Albuquerque Police Department stationary,
an eloquently worded, neatly typed
thanks-for-your-concern, but...
Fuck you
Hey man
I'm just trying to understand
I'm just trying to understand why I sleep
When stray 9mm shots wake my roommates
I'm just trying to understand why my neighbors
wanna start a Neighborhood Watch Program
I'm just trying to understand why the 7-11 clerks
in this town watch me intently after midnight
I'm just trying to understand when I ask "Why?"
to the four young Chicas with black-rimmed eyes
and sprayed up hair who're wilding the neighborhood

S L A M

Mad dogging people, jumping over fences
to take wind chimes they don't really want
or need from the looks of their fresh Starter jackets
with silver stars shimmering off the back
I reach out & ask
get my hand back burned black
They fling the chimes to the ground
when caught, spitting "I didn't want them anyways."
When I ask why they say Fuck you, man! Fuck You!
Naw, I'm just trying to understand
Why my Grampa doesn't like black people
Why he called my aunt's friend
'nigger'
told her never to bring him into his house again
I imagine the look saying
"That's how we were taught in Tennessee,
we have our place and they have theirs
and it sure as hell ain't in my house."
No, forget that
Why should I
have to explain myself to you?
I worked hard all my life,
waded into warm Pacific waters
while the Japs killed my buddies all around me
I watched my oldest son lowered into his grave
before I grew old
& now you ask me this in my own house?!!
Fuck You!
No, Grampa
I'm just trying to understand
Why I feel the twinge of hatred
after asking my sister if she's
going to keep the baby whose father is black
Wonder if the hatred is handed down
Wonder if I can cut out this cancer
given to me with my family name
When I ask that question
get my hand back burned black
the answer fuck you man

I say no man
I am just trying to...
just trying
trying to...

hold my nephew in my arms
my wet cheekbones alarm me
cause I'm afraid
afraid I'll drop him
He looks up at me
and I see in his toothless smile
that he has no fear
I see in his huge brown eyes
that he is
more than a color
more than a culture
more than any petty hatred
I see beyond all that
and I know I'm close
I know I'm beginning
to understand.

Telephone Call from Lebanon
Rifka Goldberg

Nine-thirty on Tuesday night
"Mummy, are you all right?"
"How are you?" "It is snowing"
"Are you warm enough?"
"Will you be home on Thursday?"

Something of the coldness of the snow
Seeped into the conversation
Could not help recalling
His uncalled for attack on me
When he was last at home

I did not feel the right degree of happiness
My home was not showy enough

I was not the success his father was
Remarried in a record time
Of less than nine months

Did you so quickly forget
How cruel your father was to you?
How he deprived you of money and love?
How I held on to you by the skin of my teeth
To keep you in the "family"?

Half an hour later
I realized why my son had called
Helicopter accident in the north
Seventy-three young soldiers
On their way to Lebanon, dead

I was never more grateful
At the words I had not spoken
From a home scarred not by war
To my son far away on the other end of a phone line
With whom, on that frozen night, I had held my peace

Calcium Rings
Jerry Quickley

The hills of Altadena
held the bones of
my cousin for more than a year
before hikers found him
    The animals had gotten to him
    the police said
    it must have been a drug deal gone bad
the animals had gotten to him

They shipped his remains to the family
in a box the size of a small suitcase
too small to possibly
hold his memory
or the landslides he left behind

or the pints of whiskey his father
began to swallow to keep from breaking

Lost in an urban outback
looking for anything to mute the sirens of regret
Like aborigines sniffing gasoline
stumbling towards detox farms that harvest angels

Lost histories of
dream-time and middle passages
drowned out by broken bottles
vacant lots and billy clubs

I will find myself

Lost among the vowels
creating modern mutes
looking for new metaphors
with old lies

Lost among travelers who can't hear the call
of the didjeridu
From their new homes inside of glass stems
malt liquor bottles and squeegee empires

Can you help me out with some spare change
I'm just trying to get enough for something to eat
spare change
can you
help me

Lost sounds of the prairies
a night so clear and black
the stars touch the horizon on all sides
you try to hear the earth spin
and you feel the heavens curve
with faint promises of mercy
I am so devoid of human touch
that a knee in my back
is a blessing

S L A M

I want to hurl his name into the hills
and wait for him to walk out -
whole again

I will find myself
Wandering the streets in daylight
holding a lantern   looking for one honest man

Lost among rookie cops whose idea of safe sex
is slipping a condom over their nightsticks
before using them
and throwing my cousin's bones on the floor
as though their random position
will tell the future of our tribe

Lost in the sheets   silent transfers
blood tests and first world triple cocktails

Lost among the provisions
lists of survivors
hair conditioner and film rights

Chasing ourselves into the thickets
becoming reeds to hide from ourselves
as dogs chase their tails

I will find myself

My runway is the kaleidoscope of Chavez Blvd
My prairie is the grassy expanse of traffic islands
and my cool blazed profile lying in the grass
high mesa is found on the nighttime roof of the parking
structure
where I set up my telescope   and I spy
3 Puerto Ricans from the 'hood
wiping their names on the moon's surface in petroglyphs
with cans of Krylon

And my prism tells me
there is something better
waiting for me

I will find myself
In the bones of my family
and the whispers of the hills
in the bones of my family
and the whispers of the hills

The Old Vacherie Road
Mack Dennis

A week after graduating from high school in 1958, my grandmother handed me a job announcement. It read: *FARM HANDS WANTED TWENTY-SEVEN CENTS A HOUR AND PICK UP YOUR PAYCHECK AT THE WAGUESPACK STORE.*

"But Mom!" I said to my dark skin gray headed grandmother. "That's slavery, and 'sides that, 'em a *high school graduate!*"

She squinted at me through them small, smoky black eyes and said, "Listen to me, nigga boy, when you as a baby yo' Momma didn't want you. Yo' daddy came to see you one time, and cause he got mud on his shoes, he said he wasn't coming back to the Old Vacherie Road no mo'. I been havin' you since the day you bawn. So git dat big city grin off yo' shittin' face and go sweat in da fields fo' me like I been sweatin' fo' you."

We even rode to the job site like a bunch of slaves. Black men... and black women with straw hats in a mule drawn wooden wagon driven by a snaggle toothed, instigating white man. He whacked two big brown mules with one crack of his whip and said, "Ain't no trees to shed the sun out here, school boy. Jes acres and acres of manicured brown earth and grassy green ditches. Look way over yonder where dat red tractor is plowing up dust. Dat's where we go plant sugar canes today. You can go back and tell yo' old granny dat y'all sweat go' be hot enough to boil eggs."

The plantation owners still insisted on calling them farms where we worked. But we called them slave fields. The boss man was still a white man. And even though he wouldn't shoot you if you ran, those guns boss man carried on the back window of his pick-up truck still made me nervous cause I knew I made him

SLAM

nervous by always saying, " 'Em a high school graduate!"

I sweat two years for Mom 'fore she said it was okay for me to go to New Orleans and get myself a diploma job. As I passed the sweltering field, I looked out the frosty window of the air-conditioned bus.

I saw figures bent over pulling Johnson grass out of knee high green stalks of sugar canes. I was looking for familiar faces. But all I saw was ass and elbow for *FARM HANDS WANTED TWENTY-SEVEN CENTS A HOUR AND PICK UP YOUR PAYCHECK AT THE WAGUESPACK STORE.*

Rarefied in Arkansas
Clebo Rainey

Ladies and Gentlemen! Fellow seekers of the truth!
Gather round and listen to the sound of my voice
    and the wonder of being pulled along tree lined winding
      curves
    of the Quachita Mountains between Hot Springs and
      Russelville
    on the road and gazing down on Nimrod Lake shining
    like a diamond amid the Ozarks
The sticky sap filled tips of a billion pine needles
    whip me into a whirling dervish frenzy
    twirling around and speaking in snake handling tongues
    amid the overcrowded slam pits
    reaching into the backwoods of America
    cascading impoverished notes of words hammered out on
    vocal keyboards
I peel the plastic off the Elvis CD I found at Shangri-La Records
  in Memphis
    and he blares from the speakers in my back seat
    "I hear that train a-rollin"
    "It's rollin down the line"
    "I ain't had no lovin in such a long long time"
I roll on down I-30 towards Fayetteville
    past Lee Creek
    winding along 71
    as green hills spill across my front window onto my

      dashboard
And I gotta tell ya
I am commanded by high authority to yell and tell you all
I have been rarefied in Arkansas
I must testify I have been kissed by Angels singing from
    Southern hymnals
        in Baptist and Presbyterian pews where the doubters are few
Their singing raises the ghosts of Indian spirits from the past
       and casts a spell on my right hand, once terrified
       now petrified in gold
And I am sanctified with Dixie beauty waiting in the hills of
    Arkansas
From the Cincinnati side streets I'm fleeing now
      seeing the overcrowded rundown garbage heaps
      gray housing projects
      crack addicts selling themselves on street corners
I swim in the White River in Tennessee
      stare in horror at Tommy's four floors of winding stairs
       he shares with his grape faced lover and her wine covered
        lips
I slip back on the Interstate
      send my words barreling down I-40 to Nashville to C Ra's
       poetry parlor
Mad demons filled with semen phrases too dangerous for the
    capitol country music
      stages of whiskey and beer
I fear for my safety and retreat with the confederate army across
    the mighty Mississippi
      jump on a steamer easing my way back into the Ozarks
A black crow flies low across my path where I'm sending home
    my pillow
Talkin to the moon
Wailing friends in an ocean of love
Sailin above my mountain home towards you in the blue sky
Reach for the handle
Night pen in hand
Wrapped in wet bed sheets and back on stage in Fayetteville
      where I have been rarefied in Arkansas
Ginsberg, Burroughs, Bukowski, Ferlingetti, and I retreat to the
    Quachita Mountains

and... "We won't give up"
"We won't give up"
"We'll fight"
"We'll fight"
"We'll fight"
"We've got guns"
"We've got dynamite"
"We'll fight"
"We'll fight"
"We'll fight"
Through my words pass the power
The web site of heaven opens above me in Devil's Den National
    Park
The cyber God from high reaches down towards me
A sea of stars break apart
I morph into a mad preacher in the pulpit
Start saving the terrified few who start shaking with the laying
    on of hands
Everybody stand
Start clapping your hands now
Everyone stand
Start clapping your hands now
You are saved with the glory of the Quachita Mountains
You are purified with the wet mud of the Mississippi
You are born again under the sulfur water flowin from Hot
    Springs
You are swept up in a fevered fainting passion
The world is terrified, but in Arkansas -
        in Arkansas
I tear off my clothes
I wallow in the glory of my petrified words
Slowly hands fall across my last sanctified breath where in
Arkansas -
        in Arkansas
I am rarefied

All In Its Own Time
Eva Leandersson
translated by Adele Houston

I was born in the forest far from all seas
where the moon hangs high in a fir tree
I cook my strength out of faith and dreams
filling bottles and spice with sense

I light a fire with fairytales tonight
while the lake lies black as a chimney flue
I follow a star and I tame a wild boar
collecting life as I follow the shore

SH! There's a fire-fairy in birch wood and soot
and a cat is purring on the poet's foot
there's a rising coil of smoke from our house
like a blueberry pale veil in a well curdle moon

It whispers and mumbles
between heather and moss
while the trolls fish riddles from the fairy's well
soon Mr. Jack from his pulpit will bow before little Raspberry girl
while the mist embraces a moose...

("We'll be there sometimes
playing with the rhymes
where fairytales from silent hearts
whisper through our minds
There is a place for tears
sometimes you don't know where
or how to find the magic shoes
that'll dance away your fears")

American Poets Go To Europe
Beth Lisick

The day after a wholly unsatisfying Fourth of July in San
Francisco, I flew to London to kick off a month long reading tour

with L.A. poet Jeffrey McDaniel. I've known Jeff for about five years, back when he still had bad hair and would make a production of stripping down to this ratty red muscle shirt at the climax of his performances. He's one of the most amazing poets I know, and since we'd been in a lot of weird touring situations together, I figured why not? I was about due for another random poetry trip; plus it'd be fun to be in Europe with a purpose.

No staying in youth hostels with Australians who have been travelling the world for two and a half years. We'd be crashing on the floors of our European contemporaries. Except we discovered people in Europe won't let you crash on their floors. They hand over their apartments or their mothers' apartments or a friend of their mother's apartment who is visiting relatives in the country. We'd be in London for ten days, and then head off to Germany, up to Sweden, and back down to Paris.

Here is my advice: If you are planning on doing this type of trip yourself, try to ride in on the coattails of a clean and sober dude who is incredibly organized and well-respected. It worked for me. Jeff had the whole thing dialed in advance, and I was sort of like his fun-loving drunk friend who liked to make puns in German. We were Ricky and Lucy on a foreign shore adventure, except I was the one getting uptight at him. (We did sleep in separate beds though.)

Jeff loves talking about poets and poetry constantly, which doesn't suit me so well. I got used to it after awhile, but I must say it was a relief when we rolled into a new town. Bam! There'd instantly be a fresh new face for Jeff to talk about poetry with. "Who is your favorite poet?" and "What do you think of so-and-so?" and "Have you ever heard of this guy, James Tate?" Jeff holds more poetry knowledge and opinions in his head than anyone I've ever met.

For me, the month of July was like a dream. We read to audiences ranging from 12 people to 300. We performed about 19 times and met all the groovy kids from the local scenes. I acquired a short-lived stalker and Jeff swam in a pool with rich London swingers. We sunbathed on the western shores of the "Swedish Riviera" and did our laundry across from the Notre Dame in Paris. Jeff kicked my ass at Scrabble and I kicked his ass in weird cheese-eating. We improvised with a live band in Hamburg, watched movies under the stars in Berlin, and taught workshops to kids in

Northern England. Jeff read the maps and I never, ever cared if we
got lost.

Untitled
Lynne Procope

We be pretenders,
pretenders to the position of prophet.
We don the mask of poet
late at night and between the smokes
and the lyrical jokes - we slam
up on that mic
and then just for fun
we dare to dun
the rubric of your revolution,
we stray to play the word
for audiences of the herd
prostitute the power of our pens
- in whoring for those tens

and we forget!
that this shit goes beyond gil scott
goes beyond the grand slam finals plot
this goes beyond these half-assed rhymes y'all done forgot

this art is an echo, it is a word, it is a pain,
a tear in the heart of the people
who do not have the time
to spend etching catchy lines,
when you earn under $5.25 an hour
and double up on jobs
just to buy milk or fruit or flour

this art is the lost voice of the loisaida,
plymouth rock, tienamen square, fulton street and death row
because we will never know
what we have lost
if our poets don't tell us about the linear nature of our oppressors
if our poets don't re-write the riot act and the miranda advisement

S L A M

- we have no right & no reason to remain silent
we must rage a joyful, powerful, angry noise
if we remain silent
they believe that they have won
anything we say must speak to truth
- the innocents are listening
can and will must be our watchwords
    we must watch words
    before they can be held against us
- or taken away from us
poet and humanity
must hold each other and remember

that our revolution has not been televised
    it must not be demonized
    it must not been marginalized
    and it never basketball!
        and this is not a remix!

this art is a coming home,
a reclaiming of boriqua land ,
a relearning the ghost dance of black elk
because the language and rhythms of our ancestors
died a little bit,
every day they were silenced.
is the trial by fire of militant ire
the art of spoken word -
goes beyond conjugation of the verb

it is the invocation to act

the evolution of thought

and the way we know that we are not alone,

poet - did you read fanon, shakur or any one of the barakas
did you ever cry when willie told how petey died?
did fela ever make you stamp or rudder make you shine
or marley make you lift you head to jah on high?
did you read? Have you listened?
Do you know the definition

of your revolution...
Or are you just pretendin' when you step up to the mic?

I Don't Want to Slam
Staceyann Chin

I've decided
I don't want to be
a poet who just writes
for the slam anymore

I want to stop writing
poor excuses for poems
that do nothing but
stroke my ego and fool
the crowd into thinking
my bucking and screaming
was actually their orgasm

I don't want to be a poet
writing to slam anymore

I don't want
to join the staged revolution
don't want to be a part of just
some spotlight-slamming solutions
don't want to go to Austin or Chicago
simply because I think I have
the rapidly moving metaphors
smashing off the Nuyorican walls
or similes like a silver bullet
bee-lining for the finals on a balloon
full of nothing but hot air
making the room smell like a fart
from a bad poem that somebody
should have said excuse me for

I don't want to just slam anymore

S L A M

I don't want to sit
in smoke-filled rooms
listening to women who rhyme
creating lyrics that rock
making sure they fit within
the confines of some judge's ticking clock
smiling with people I've only seen
on the corner of an old SlamNation flyer
trying to get them to tell me
how to record that first CD
how to really work a crowd
how to fuck those hard to please judges
so I can give birth to a bastard TEN

I'm tired of igniting blazes on the mike
pimping poems about my lover's private life
sipping iced tea over superlatives
eating spring rolls over hyperboles
juxtapositioning myself in vegetarian cafes
between guys with funny sounding names
like Guy and Procope and Dot
hoping some of what makes them real poets
will rub off on a pretender like me

I want to be like them
when I finally grow up
because I've watched them
rewrite stolen histories
in breathtaking three minute pieces
doing only honest performances
so that every time they go on
they kick a poem with heart
fighting the fanfare of this
slamming psuedo-revolution
changing the world
one poem at a time

Now that I've actually been a poet
been romantic and been poor
I don't want to be a slam poet anymore

Today I want to write
from a place where I change lives
and change people and places
cross over boundaries
of sexes and cultures and races
paint the skies deep red
instead of boring blue
write the true histories of me and you
crawl deep inside the lines
of every poem I write
I want to speak about the stars
as if I had become the night

Tonight I want to be
intimate with my muse
Hell - I want to bed the woman
I want to have her so close
she gets up inside me
so when I am asleep
she can rouse me
No!
I want her to arouse me
have her way with me
have her play with me
so that when I wake up
I will be inspired
to write honest poems
poems about grandmothers
and babies and truth
poems that don't care
about the meter or the rhyme
poems that really couldn't give
a flying fuck about the time
poems that will not sit
within the squares of any chart
poems that are written in blood
flowing straight from the heart

I want to write

S L A M

I left my lover and
now I want her back poems
I miss Jamaica
but I'm never going back poems
I know it's not a ten
but it sends shivers down MY back poems
poems that talk about life
and love and laughter
poems that reveal the flaws
that make up strikingly real people
real poems
poems that are so honest
they slam

At The Slam
Steve Marsh

After I had paid my cover charge,
And bought beer enough
To wash away the performance anxiety.
The ten dollar prize
Left me just two-fifty in the hole,
Plus tip.

My Pain Keeps Me Regular
Edward Thomas Herrera

My pain
My pain
My pain

My pain is better than anyone else's
my pain is more serious than anyone else's
my pain is more important than anyone else's

Compared to my pain
everyone else's pain is petty
everyone else's pain is meaningless

everyone else's pain is a day at the beach a walk in the park a
    fucking
piece of fucking cake
it's my pain
my pain
my pain
my pain

my pain beating breasts
my pain licking open sores
my pain crying thick red tears of arterial blood
my pain twisting the knife blade around and around and around
my pain representative of all the injustice that ever happened is
happening
or will happen to anyone anywhere anyhow

My pain
My pain
My pain

I blame my lovers
I blame my parents
I blame organized religion
I blame the current administration
I blame the capitalist system of economics

But most importantly
I blame everyone who has ever lived
because they have all been party to my torment
if not directly
then indirectly
if you don't believe me
just give me a little time
I can find blood on your hands
somehow somewhere some way

trust me

My pain
My pain

S L A M

My pain

Some say I need to get over it transcend
some say I need to put it all behind me go on with my life
some say I may require professional help in order to accomplish
   all this

but what do they know
they've never experienced my pain
my pain is so truly enormously unique
if I don't dwell on it then just who would

My pain
My pain
My pain

Boy howdy does the world owe me but big time

My pain
My pain
My pain

My pain
allows me to be bitter and resentful
  towards those who have caused my suffering
  towards those who do not share my suffering
  towards those who have not heard about my suffering
my pain
releases me from the responsibility
of having to accomplish something with my life
because I can always blame my failure on my status
as a member of a socially disenfranchised group of people
my pain
makes me the most important person in this room
  and if you don't agree
  that's because you don't understand
  and there's something horribly horribly wrong with you

Thank you

P O E T R Y

Head To Head Haiku
Daniel Ferri

The first time Head to Head Haiku happened at the Nationals was in Ann Arbor, 1995. We picked the haikuster's names out of a paper bag. I stood on the stage, wearing a shirt and nail-belt dyed red, and the other side their original not-red. In the red nail-belt pocket were nine red wooden balls. Nine not-red balls were in the other pocket. A piece of painted 1x4 wood with two dowels poking up was stuck in my belt, onto which I slipped the red and not-red balls to keep track of the score. The judges waved bamboo sticks with red and not-red duct tape on the ends for flags. The red haikuster wore a red headband, the not-red haikuster had the sleeve from one of my old tee-shirts on his head.

The haikusters kept wanting to introduce their haiku. A sharp "Read Fucking Haiku" dissuaded most of them. Everyone was goofing and laughing, but soon things quieted down. One poem read, silence, then the next haiku answered it like a batter's swing answers a pitch. Then the judges vote for red or not-red by raising their flags. The red ball, or the not-red ball clacks on the dowel and we read again. Best three out of five wins the round.

The space took on a quiet rhythm. The silent spaces between and within each poem let us hear each syllable of the haiku.

Then it was the finals. Best nine of seventeen in the finals. One poet ran out of haiku and tried repeating ones he'd done already. The judges were having none of it. He turned to me and, asked what he should do. Someone called from the audience, "Make 'em up!" So he did. Counting syllables on his fingers, losing count, the audience calling out suggestions, cheering when he found a good word, a fine turn. It was like everyone in the room was making the poems.

The other poet won the match. If we lived in a perfect world there would be no difference between who won and who didn't, but since we don't the champion was awarded $17, one for each syllable of the ancient and venerated poetry form we had just eviscerated.

S L A M

Safety
Aaron Yamaguchi

As the plane nose dived
the kamikaze pilot
tightened his helmet

Haiku
DJ Renegade

Basketball game ends
Breathing hard I bend over;
Ants carry a leaf

Blues is the color
Of a punctured heart
Bleeding across guitar strings

Jazz is the way
Brown sugar would sound if it
Was sprinkled in your ear

Spirituals are how
Angles would sound singing
In a cotton field

Haiku
Deborah Edler Brown

She writes in crayon:
"You cannot be mean to me!"
Her sword is purple.

Haiku
Kimberly Jordan

I shudder to think
of myself in an office
playing solitaire

POETRY

Group Discussion on the Group Piece
*Mike Henry, Karyna McGlynn, Danny Solis, Susan
B. Anthony Somers-Willett, Genevieve Van Cleve,
Hilary Thomas, Phil West, and Wammo*

The group piece grew out of the whole team concept of national competition. If four people band together to form a team, the thinking went, why not take advantage and allow the poets to collaborate in writing and performance? Since the 1991 Nationals, when the Chicago team presented a group piece in competition, duos, trios, and quartets have become an integral part of numerous teams' poetic arsenals. They have not only become a key facet of many teams' strategies, but have also provided teams with the chance to learn each of its members' voices in a more intimate, creative, and cooperative manner. This discussion highlights the thrills and dangers of scripting, preparing, and delivering multi-voiced poems.

Mike: I remember putting together our first group piece in '95. It was going to be our first Nationals and we had no idea what we were doing.

Phil: Wammo told us it'd be a good idea to have a group piece. It hadn't really occurred to us before. We formed our team, like, three weeks before Nationals.

Mike: We showed up for one of our few rehearsals and Wammo said, "Okay, Pony, you do 'Motor Red' and Mike and I will make car noises and act like we're driving. Gen, you'll smoke, look pissed off and wait for your cue to say 'Asshole.' It'll be great."

Phil: Oddly enough, it was. We performed it to 300 people, a completely packed room, and they went absolutely nuts at the end of the piece. And then, the next night, we saw Asheville win the finals on the strength of solid group work. They'd scripted Danny Solis's 'Every Day' into a quartet that took advantage of each one of their voices. There was such a gorgeous, orchestrated, choral calamity to the piece.

214

Gen: Pretty much all hell breaks loose. It's my favorite part of being on a slam team. The beauty part of the whole deal is that people bust their ass to make something bigger or different than themselves.

Susan: I can't rave enough about how enriching collaboration can be. Yes, it's hard, and yes, you have to deal with everybody's ego...

Wammo: Usually, I have a few brilliant ideas and then everybody else shuffles along.

Susan: ...but the product is usually better than anything you could have written alone.

Danny: The variety and richness of the group poem, as it has evolved in the milieu of the slam, is unprecedented.

Phil: When you're competing to win a spot on your city's team, you're typically very focused on yourself. The prospect of preparing a group piece, once you make the team, gives you the opportunity to learn about the other people on your team - intimately.

Mike: The process can happen in many ways: the entire team writing on agreed-upon topics and melding work together, or looking for existing poems that lend themselves to multiple voices.

Karyna: Group pieces can evolve from retired solo pieces that have long since been abandoned.

Mike: I've even seen cases where two separate poems written by different team members can be married together.

Phil: I'm partial to writing together, the whole ritual -

Mike: Passing a laptop computer back and forth across the table -

Phil: Getting into a rhythm where you're writing in this sort of shared voice -

Mike: And when the piece is finished, it is often difficult to trace back to what single idea or image was the starting point.

Phil: Or to even trace who came up with what. In '97, when we did "Personal Ads," I came up with the original concept, but it was really all of us sitting around Susan's place one night, coming up with lines, including ones we'd said in other contexts months before. For instance, Gen hosted a slam earlier that year where Karyna had done a poem about being a dangerous, sexy Scorpio, and when Gen got back on stage, she said, in this really funny bleating voice, "I'm a Caaaapricorn. All I have to offer you is grass and garbage. Hope you stick around." We worked that in.

Gen: Epic discussions have taken place over the placement of a phrase or an article - whether to use 'or' or 'and' in a passage. We passionately champion the smallest swords so that our meaning is clear and the power or beauty or humor in our work is unmistakable.

Mike: Four poets become one voice.

Karyna: It's hard to be a team player and give valuable input when you utterly detest the idea for the group piece that's being written. If your experience with the subject is painful while everyone else's is humorous, you have to make a hard choice: tell the awful truth, or make up something lighter and easier to read.

Gen: There are two important, crucial points in the life of a group piece. The first is the moment in the writing phase of the project where it finally seems like a poem. The second point is during rehearsal. A group piece has a way of being an absolute disaster and a pain in the ass until the magic moment in rehearsal where the group figures out what it's supposed to look like.

Phil: Early on, you're just slogging through, seeing if the piece actually holds together as a poem, but then, you get little breakthroughs.

Mike: Happy accidents.

Phil: In "Personal Ads," we had this section where Gen and Wammo say, "Take a chance, call," and Susan follows with a breathy, sexy, "Take a chance, call." In one practice, she was goofing around and did this come-hither facial gesture at the end of the line that we've since come to know as "the lip thing." That's the moment we truly realized we had a lot of room to play.

Gen: In those rehearsals we discovered together that Susan was a brilliant physical comedian. She didn't know.

Karyna: When Susan, Gen, and I got together to freewrite on "Daddy" in 1998, it all came out, and almost pieced itself together. After we read the rough draft aloud for the first time, we all just looked around at each other with a few tears in our eyes, nodding, and going, "Yeah ... yeah." It just worked. Working with just two other women, I was much more honest.

Susan: The poem seemed to take forever in process, but the result of it was something of which we were extremely proud. The three of us became closer as teammates, and this reflected even more in our performance.

Gen: I believe audiences can sense true collaboration and reward the effort. I think pieces that come from a selfish or uneven collaborative effort look funny - you can hear the direction of one voice leading the others. While these poems may work sometimes, a good audience can sense a fox in the chicken coop.

Danny: In the course of a regular evening of slamming, the audiences see one poet after another. Individual voices, even if they are excellent, are still just individual voices. When a good group poem comes along, it connects the team with the audience in a way that an individual poem cannot.

Susan: For me, the group piece best exemplifies the benefits of slam poetry over the written word. Not only does a poet get to "embody" his or her work - give the poem a voice, a body, a physical expression - but a group piece gives a poem several different voices.

Gen: It is a break from the traditional image of the poet - one voice, one body, one microphone.

POETRY

Danny: A good group piece multiplies voices instead of just adding them.

Susan: With a group, a poet can give a poem a rhythm and pace that is impossible when he or she reads it alone.

Danny: It differs from an indie poem in obvious ways - visually, sonically, verbally - and in ways that are not so tangible. I firmly believe that the process pushes our art forward, farther into the light of realizing its true potential.

Mike: One way to look at it is that instead of one single person for the audience to identify with, laugh with, cry with, there are two or three or four. More for the audience to experience. Like in "Super Heroes" by the 1998 Dallas team. That poem would be fantastic performed by any one of the individual voices, but when the audience hooks into the three performers, the universality of the ideas becomes more pronounced. Plus it just fuckin' rocks.

Danny: Everyone likes "Super Heroes" because it's funny, but at the same time it is a very serious poem about identity and self-image.

Hilary: The group piece helps bring teams together.

Gen: It binds us, it challenges your creative process and personal boundaries. How can you not care about those that you've given birth with - crafted, doubted, sweated and nurtured with?

Hilary: You must trust your teammates with your baby, your idea, your poem.

Gen: If it is a serious piece that requires the participants to lay themselves bare, you do not take that journey alone. You learn about your co-creators in a profoundly deep and intimate way. If it is a humorous piece, you celebrate and nurture each other and the work.

Mike: One of my favorite elements of group work is that it creates opportunities for poets to work outside of their "comfort zone" - to perform in ways that they wouldn't otherwise.

Hilary: You will stretch muscles you didn't know you had.

Phil: Group work has definitely given me the courage to integrate potentially embarrassing physicalizations into my own solo work, and it taught me that, even if it is uncomfortable at first, it's golden if you place it right, as the audience gets to see how far you're willing to go.

Danny: Any poet can memorize a poem for an audience, but it takes a special sensibility to take a good poem and script it in a way that brings more into and out of the poem than would be possible for one voice.

Mike: Some people seem to think that they can just divide up the lines and read the poem. There's more to it than that. You have to look at the text as a map.

Danny: And serve the poem.

Mike: And let it show you how to stop being four individuals and become one collaborative voice.

Danny: A bad group piece just adds voices to add volume.

Phil: Even the simplest arrangement of four people in a line somehow has to transcend that arrangement, or everyone besides the author becomes extraneous. It's not hard to tell when a team hasn't worked a piece hard enough.

Karyna: In '99, with our four-person group piece, we had to address issues of whether our voices would carry in the space we were going to read in, and whether we would trip over each other's microphone wires while running back and forth. We realized, just before the competition, that hand-holding the mikes was difficult for all of us, and messed up our voice dynamics.

Phil: And rather than risk doing a piece we weren't ready to do, we scrapped it.

Susan: It seems that when they aren't done well or when the audience isn't ready for one, they seriously bomb. I think an audience is much more offended by a group espousing bad poetry than just one person, like, "Why did four (or three, or two) people think this was a good idea?"

Mike: Group work can be a tremendous strategic tool in a team bout if you use it right.

Wammo: Some teams make the mistake of doing too many group pieces at the finals and it's all my fault.

Phil: For the '96 finals, we decided to feature our group work as much as possible.

Mike: Three out of four rotations.

Phil: We were proud of those group pieces. The judges tanked us, even though many poets in the audience were screaming for their heads. We forgot, in our excitement, that the group piece is highly specialized, and requires strong individual work to correctly frame it. Still, poets came up to me after finals and praised us for taking that risk.

Danny: It allows the team a greater variety of options during a bout. And if community is what the slam is really all about, then a good group piece conceived and executed by a team can be a microcosmic reflection of a community working in harmony, putting individual egos aside and creating something new that is greater than the sum of its parts.

Super Hero, Baby
GNO, Jason Edwards, Jason Carney

GNO:
Look, up in the sky, it's a bird, it's a plane, it's a bad mother...
"Shut yo mouth!"
I'm just talking about my black super hero, baaaby!
When I was a kid, I wanted to be a superhero, a black superhero.

SLAM

My mama use to pin a big ol' beach towel around my neck
I would put on my red cowboy boots and in an instant:
I was black and strong, black and intelligent, black and beautiful.
I was a black super hero, baaaaby!
I was the original Lone Ranger, before he got with Tonto
I wouldn't be swinging through your neighborhood
Like that silly fool in tights, Spiderman. Oh noooo!
I was more like, "The Black Tarantula!"
I would even cruise the mean city streets in my Blackmobile
While keeping the fuzz in check!
I possessed the super black gift of gab, reciting Malcolm X
    speeches to the
Uninformed by any means necessary
I was bad, I was cool,
I would even shoot soooooooooooooooul power out of my black
    power fist Afro
pick.
My theme music consisted of songs like
"I'm Black and I'm Proud" by James Brown, "Respect" by Aretha
    Franklin, and
"Chocolate City" by Parliament-Funkedelic.

Jason Carney:
Look up in the sky it's a bird it's a plane it's a bad mother...
"Shut yo' mouth!"
I'm just talkin' bout my redneck super hero baaaby!
When I was a child I always wanted to be a super hero
Not just any super hero, but a red neck superhero.
I would lower the back of my Wranglers to expose butt crack
Don myself in black and walked with the swagger of Johnny Cash
Spewed out the verbiage of a Roscoe P. Coltrane
And possessed the dynamic good looks of Willie Nelson
My fortress would be a steel reinforced doublewide trailer
Impenetrable even to the fiercest of tornadoes
I would cruise the rural back roads of mesquite
In my primered out 1976 Ford 4x4
Squashing the most uneducated of degenerates thieves muggers
And people who say they ain't even Christians
And then paralyzing them with the toxic juices I spit
with the help of my Red Man chew

And after a long day's haul I would hanker down with my six-pack
Of Coors and enjoy my theme song "Good Friends, Good
    Whiskey, and Good Lovin"
Yeah man I would be a red neck super hero

Jason Edwards:
Look up in the sky it's a bird it's a plane it's a bad mother...
"Shut yo' mouth!"
I'm just talkin' bout my gay super hero baaaby!
When I was a kid, I wanted to be a superhero, a fashionable one
I would steal my big sister's Wonder Woman underoos
Pin her 1970s Bugaloo wings to my back
Take her fairy wand in hand and then waa-bam!!!
I was a gay superhero baaaby!
Oh I was so original redecorating homes in a single bound
Girl please Martha Stewart ain't got nothin on this bitch
I was Flawless, I was Fabulous
I would shoot queeeeeer power like sequence and gold lamé out
    of my blowdryer
cruisin the mall in my new Versace, keepin my boyz in check!
Hey Now!!! Hey Now!!!
My theme music was
"Vogue" by Madonna
"Express Yourself" by Madonna
and "Like a Virgin" by Madonna

Together:
No longer would the man oppress my people
No longer would bad bleach jobs go on ignored
Someone to save the day
Someone to take the pain away
Someone to kick your racist ass
For I was... I am and shall continue to be
A black gay redneck
Super Hero baaaby !!!

S L A M

Saying It with Meat/Duet
Gregory Hischak

Eve: When I thought you were stalking me, you broke the ice with an 8 oz. flank steak.

Adam: An old lover's flank steak left in my freezer.

Eve: You left it outside my apartment along with an Omaha Steaks catalog.

Adam: The mailman left in my box by mistake.

Eve: I was moved.

Adam I was encouraged.

Eve: When your parking invaded my personal space, you apologized with four Chicken Parmesan Patties.

Adam: Chicken elegantly dusted with spices of Old Italy.

Eve: I invited you to dinner.

Adam: We had dinner.

Both: Chicken.

Eve: When you got sick on my couch,

Adam: I made it up to you with a breast of Lamb Kiev.

Eve: It was to die for.

Adam: Things were really going pretty well.

Eve: When my grandpa passed away unexpectedly, you consoled me with Triple-Trimmed Filet Mignons.

Adam: Corn fed fillets, carefully aged and selected for

tenderness, hand-trimmed, flash frozen and shipped all the way
from Omaha Steak's...

Eve: ...temperature-controlled warehouse.
Adam: Exactly.

Eve: When you said that you loved me, but really didn't, you
said it with Hardwood-Smoked Veal Sausages.

Adam: The unmistakably delicate taste of veal stuffed with
tempestuous spices in five tantalizing flavors.

Eve: You said you weren't ready for this kind of commitment.

Adam: And I said it with Boneless Center Chops.

Eve: Cuts impossible to find in restaurants—

Adam: Available only from Omaha Steaks.

Eve: When you finally left me, you left me with an 8 oz. rib rack
in my freezer—

Adam: Ribs

Eve: Cut from the heart of the short loin.

Adam: I thought it would be a nice gesture.

Eve: There was never a time when you were honest with me.

Adam: It's the corn feeding — that's the secret to truly
spectacular meat. Corn-feeding gives the meat a wonderful
interior marbling that dissolves during cooking. I've always tried
to be honest with you, except for that one.

Eve: Two

Adam: Three times when I could have told you I was a...

Both: Vegetarian,

Adam: but didn't

Eve: I knew all along

Adam: And you could have said something.

Eve: But I didn't.

Eve: We've always found ways to circumvent saying the things that needed to be said.

Adam: I've always tried to say it with meat.

Eve: When something needed to be said.

Adam: I said it with meat.

Eve: Bacon-wrapped London Broil, Lemon Tarragon Chicken, Chateaubriand Corn-beef Brisket, Bone-in Spiral Sliced Ham, Double Loin Lamb Chops, Cajun-Breaded Veal T-bones. You've strung me along.

Adam: I've strung you along with Hardwood-smoked Veal Sausages.

Eve: Tempestuous spices.

Adam: Tantalizing flavors.

Eve: We were living a lie.

Adam: We were lying from the heart.

Eve: We were living a lie. We were lying

Adam: with all the best cuts available.

Group Sex
Regie Cabico, Evert Eden, Taylor Mali, Beau Sia

Taylor: The first time I ever made love...
Evert: My cherry was mauled...
Beau: Penthouse Forum come true...
Regie: When I lost my...
All: VIRGINITY!
Taylor: It was...
Beau: I was...
Taylor: It was...
Beau: I was...
Taylor: It was...
Beau: I was fantastic!
Evert: Oh, the horror.
Regie: Oh, the size! Scene 1: A gay bar late one night...
Taylor: Both of our parents were out of town for the weekend...
Beau: I had just run 10 miles...
Evert: I had just puked all over my shoes...
Taylor: It was the summer after our sophomore year...
Regie: I was a sophomore in college...
Evert: It was skunk hour in a topless bar...
Beau: It was the entire 8th grade girls' volleyball team...
Taylor: We were high school sweethearts and we'd been...
Evert: We were total strangers
All: YOU HAVE NO IDEA WHAT IT'S LIKE
        TO BE A GAY FILIPINO IN A LEATHER BAR!

Regie: His name was David
Beau: Their names were Nadine, Eileen, Cindy, Veronica...
Evert: Jabba the Slut
Taylor: Jennifer, our parents knew each other
Regie: More like Da-veeeed
Taylor: She led me up to her parents' bedroom.
Regie: He led me into his alley
Evert: She hauled me into the toilet
Taylor: There were candles everywhere and soft music playing
Regie: It smelled like stale beer
Evert: It smelled like shit
Taylor: I drowned in her skies.

Regie: He squeezed my butt and for a moment
All: Everything felt so good.
Evert: Bad
All: Everything felt so right.
Evert: Wrong
All: Everything was bliss.
Evert: Shit
Regie: His hands
Evert: My hands
Taylor: Whose hands?
Beau: Sixteen pairs of hands, like that Indian dude...
    [All stand behind Taylor and wave arms]
All: SHIVA!
Beau: Hands everywhere.
Taylor: Clutching at clothes
Regie: I unbuckled his belt
Beau: They all took off their letter sweaters
Evert: She went for my zipper
Taylor: I took off her shirt
Beau: All those little bobbi socks
Evert: Two breasts
Regie: Two cocks
Taylor: Two hearts
Evert: Two moles
Regie: Too hard
Beau: 32 pompoms
Taylor: All the stars in her eyes
Beau: And thank God they still had their knee pads on
Regie: I got on my knees [Regie kneels down]
Taylor: She knelt down before me
Evert: She rolled down my foreskin like pantyhose
Beau: We went through every page of "The Joy of Beau"
    [Beau starts assuming various positions and yelling out page
numbers]
Taylor: I knew what I wanted her to do
Regie: I knew what I had to do
Evert: What was she going to do?
Taylor: She took me in her mouth and
Regie: Oh man!
Taylor: Oh boy!
Evert: Oh No!

Regie: Oh Jesus!
Taylor: Oh God!
Evert: Oh Shit!
Regie: Isus Meriosep! (This is apparently Filipino for Jesus
           Christ)
Taylor: Jennifer!
Evert: Oh Fuck!
Regie: His cock melted in my mouth
Taylor: She was sucking my cock like the movies
Evert: She mangled my meat.
Regie: It was like a microphone
Taylor: It was incredible
Evert: It was awful
Regie: Mmmmmmm
Taylor: Oooooooooooo
Evert: ouch!
Beau: Yesssssss!
Regie: Mmmmmmm
Taylor: Oooooooooooo
Evert: ouch!
Beau: Yessssss!
Regie: It's time
All: It's time, it's time, it's time
Beau: What time is it?
Taylor: It's time to make love
Evert: It's time to do the nasty
Regie: It's time to get busy
Beau: It's time to get my dong on!
Taylor: You know, do it.
Evert: Bleed the Lizard!
Regie: Do the Jello dance
Beau: Let's get physical
Taylor: Have sex
Evert: Bury the foaming beef probe.
Regie: Copulate the Montague
Beau: Share my gift with the world!
    [All perform rhythmic beat-box sex chant until final mind-
blowing group orgasm!]

S L A M

Tube
Danny Solis, Hilary Thomas, Wammo, Phil West

Danny: We interrupt your regularly scheduled program to bring you this
Phil: Refreshing
Wammo: Gunfire
Hilary: Fabulous
Danny: Odor
Wammo: New and improved
Phil: Act of cowardice
Danny: Minty-fresh
Hilary: Bloodshed
Phil: A must for those who are dieting
Wammo: You can't find a better set of knives
Hilary: The death toll continues to rise
Danny: Now available on home video
Phil: Free with each box of
Wammo: Massive environmental destruction
Hilary: He scores
Danny: He could go all the way
Phil: He draws the foul
Wammo: This game is over

Phil: Rounding out the top five movies for the week were "Rocky XII" starring Sylvester Stallone and "Weekend At Bernie's III."
Hilary: When one helping just isn't enough, try Family-Sized Stove Top
Danny: death count in Rwanda continues to rise as over a hundred children a day perish from starvation and malnutrition-related diseases.
Wammo: And the Lord Almighty Jehovah shall rain down a great fire upon those who would transgress against his precious flock
All: No Americans were killed in the disaster.

Phil: Moving on to national news
Hilary: There's so many ways to fix beef
Wammo: You're soaking in it.

Danny: I'm not your uncle, Sylvia. I'm your father
Phil: There's an awful lot riding on this putt
Danny: Affirmative action
Hilary: Mandate
Wammo: Lemony
Phil: Boycott
Hilary: No comment
Danny: No comment
Wammo: No money down
Phil: No credit - no problem
Hilary: No product on the market works better to insure
Phil: Eight hours of hair-raising
Phil & Danny: watch it and you die a thousand deaths
Wammo: terror-drenched, blood-curdling horror film
Hilary: at 11
Danny: with our brand-new sky cam bringing you the latest
Wammo: miracle of modern technology

Phil: Now here's Sandra with sports
Hilary: In football news today, a bunch of steroid-laden
        machoids pranced around in stupid-looking costumes
        trying to prove what big men they are in a grandiose
        display of latent homosexual male contact-oriented
        grunting
Danny: And for more football news, let's go to Steve
Wammo & Phil: at the courthouse
Hilary: where we've had reporters working all day

Phil: According to police spokesmen, the internal
        investigation concluded the shooting was accidental.
        The 17-year-old black male suspect is still in serious but
        stable condition
Danny: But your guests will not have to worry about that
        unpleasantness - all they'll see is the nice centerpiece
        you put together for your small but elegant dinner
Wammo: And now Barbara, if you can tell us which would cost
        more, the deodorant or the peas, you'll win the
        fabulous, all-expenses paid trip to Tierra Del Fuego!
Hilary: The real thing
Phil: The death toll

S L A M

Wammo & Danny: A BRAND NEW CAR!

Phil & Hilary: Good and good for you

Danny: Here's Dick with the weather

Wammo: STAY IN YOUR HOMES

Phil: And order pay-per-view for the Wrestling Poetry
          SUDDEN-DEATH CAGE MATCH OF THE
          CENTURY.

Wammo: He lost his belt to Robert "Iron John" Bly in
          SuperSlamaBama III and he's not about to forget it.

Danny: [Improv as insane poet wrestler]

Hilary: If we get close, and he smells, forget it.

Phil: So we're back at the MTV Beach House to

Danny: wreak havoc

Wammo: and let the angel with the flaming sword cut loose the
          bonds of sin. Let's check the current contribution totals
          for this evening, shall we?

Phil/Danny/Hilary: No Americans were killed in the disaster.

Wammo: Hallelujah!

Phil: The new breakthrough AIDS treatment will cost
          patients anywhere from 40 to 60 thousand dollars a year

Wammo: And we will be saved

Danny: More fighting today in the West Bank

Wammo: By the power of Jesus

Hilary: This brought to you by

Wammo: Our almighty Lord, who looks upon us and says

Phil: We'll get back to warm and sunny weather by Friday

Hilary: Just in time for the weekend

Wammo: And in tomorrow's news

Danny: based on an analysis of current global trends

Hilary: looking toward the future

Phil: A team of experts have predicted

Danny: our civilization will soon be

All: STATIC

Redheads
Tim Sanders and Gabrielle Bouliane

Gabrielle (sings to the tune of "Sometimes It's Hard To Be A
Woman"): "Sometimes it's hard to be a redhead..."

Tim: Growing up, you're half Norman Rockwell, half Campbell's
soup kid, ya got rosy cheeks and dreams of distant Irelands while
kids all hollered,
Gabrielle: CARROT TOP!
Tim: Aren't carrot tops green?
Gabrielle: Amen, brother!
Tim: Growing up, you're always in trouble, it's a goddamn
conspiracy, oh the redhead did it, it was their fault, they were the
leader, not those
Gabrielle: Blond
Tim: Brunette
Gabrielle: Beautiful
Tim: Buttered-up
Gabrielle: Boys and girls
Tim: Boys and girls.
Gabrielle: They had *two* seats in the principal's office,
Tim: One for redheads,
Gabrielle: One for everybody else. I came to know that seat like
a second home, came to know the phonecalls my parents
received almost daily...
Tim: "Hello? Mrs. Bouliane? This is Mr. Smithers over at
Lincoln Elementary, it seems your daughter has set fire to my
new Maverick again.
Gabrielle: I *did* do that.
Tim: You should have seen the flames. It was poetry.
Gabrielle: Growing up, you get to the birds and the bees.
Tim: Coming out of puberty like a bottle rocket, I recall looking
down in the shower one twelve-year-old morning to discover,
Gabrielle: Sprouting, like spring clover, <*pop!*>
Tim: A strawberry patch.
Gabrielle: Then came high school...
Both: *Whooooooo*
Tim: I recall scenes on the couch, with the shirts off and the
pants coming undone,

Gabrielle: And when it came to slipping off the undies,
(Both grab like pulling up pants with a scared face)
Tim: That's what I'm talking about,
Gabrielle: There was fear!!
Tim: Anxiety!
Gabrielle: 'Cause you didn't know how to warn them
Tim: And you felt that you *had* to warn them
Gabrielle: That there's *fire* in this crotch!
(Bump hips)
Tim: But we were just trying to add a little color to the world, all those dull shades, those drab colors, no passion, no life, no desire...
Gabrielle: no
Tim: Red!
Both: VIVA LA REDHEADS Manifesto!
Tim: I want to wake to a *red* dawn, climb into my little *red* Corvette, pick up Little Red Riding Hood, ask her if she's *red* any good books lately, and drive into the *Red* Sea, where they'll find us, simply *red*
Gabrielle: I wanna wake up, smear red dye #5 on my lips, take my little red wagon down to the red light district, hang out with Red Skelton eating red herring and cutting through every single piece of red tape they try to lay around us...
Tim: You see, a spoonful of red
Gabrielle: Helps *everything* go down!
Tim: Red as roses,
Both: 'cause we're blooming
Gabrielle: Red as fire engines,
Both: 'cause we haul ass
Tim: Red as blood,
Both: 'cause we know when to PUMP and when to trickle down
Gabrielle: Red as fever, 'cause
Tim: "We'll give ya fever, baby" - Red as stop signs, because you must stop
Both: And dig it
Gabrielle: Red as Valentine's Day, 'cause we're, well,
Tim: Tender and shit.
Gabrielle (sung): "Sometimes it's hard to be a redhead, giving your love to just one slam, but if you love it, hold onto it, 'cause after all, it's just a slam.."

Tim (spoken simultaneously): We're the redheaded stepchilds, the crazy freckled fuckers playing banjo on the porch, the sunburned devils, the blue eyes and the hot temper, mess with us and you'll wish you wound up —
Both: *red.*

Poetry Slam: A Timeline

1984. Construction worker and poet Marc Smith starts a poetry reading series at a Chicago jazz club, the Get Me High Lounge, looking to breathe life into the open mike poetry format. The series' emphasis on performance lays the groundwork for the poetry slam.

1986. Smith approaches Dave Jemilo, owner of the Green Mill (a Chicago jazz club and former haunt of Al Capone), with a plan to host a weekly poetry competition on the club's slow Sunday nights. On July 25, the Uptown Poetry Slam is born. Smith draws on baseball and bridge terminology for the name, and institutes the basic features of the competition, including judges chosen from the audience and cash prizes for the winners. The Green Mill evolves into a mecca for performance poets, and the Uptown Poetry Slam still continues every Sunday.

1987-90. Ann Arbor, Michigan's slam begins in August 1987; New York begins slamming in 1989. San Francisco and Anchorage, Alaska follow in 1990. New York's home base, the Nuyorican Poets Cafe in the East Village, becomes one of the best-known homes for slam.

1990. The first-ever National Poetry Slam is produced by Gary Mex Glazner on October 18 in San Francisco, featuring four-person teams from Chicago and San Francisco and an individual poet from New York. The Chicago team wins the debut team competition, and Chicago's Patricia Smith wins the individual competition.

1991. Chicago hosts a national competition featuring teams from eight cities, including Boston, Cleveland and the first team from New York. Organizer Marc Smith coins the term National Poetry Slam to promote the event. The Chicago team repeats as champion and premieres the first-ever group piece in Nationals competition, with Lisa Buscani as individual champion. The three-minute time rule is introduced, including an on-stage clock. While the three-minute rule still remains, the on-stage clock does not.

1992. Seventeen cities are represented at the Nationals in Boston by team or individual competitors; the first-ever Native American slam team is among the 12 teams competing. Boston wins - the second year in a row the host city has done so.

1993. San Francisco hosts the Nationals in which 23 teams compete, including the first teams from Canada (Victoria, B.C.), Europe (Finland), Seattle, Portland, Los Angeles, and Washington, D.C. For the first time, side events including the haiku slam, the sonnet slam, erotic and midnight non-competitive readings become part of the festivities. Boston and Patricia Smith repeat as champions.

1994. The Fifth National Poetry Slam is held in Asheville, North Carolina, won by the Cleveland team and individual competitor Gayle Danley, representing Atlanta. Allan Wolf coins the phrase, "The points are not the point; the point is poetry." Meanwhile, poet Juliette Torrez coordinates the Lollapalooza tour poetry stage, exposing new audiences to spoken word performance. As a result, a number of slams start up, particularly in the Southwest and on the West Coast.

1995. Ann Arbor hosts the Nationals with 27 teams participating, including Austin, Dallas, Detroit, Athens, GA, Key West, FL, and Albuquerque. Organizers Steve and Deb Marsh introduce computerized scoring and the three-team bout, a departure from the head-to-head competition of previous National Poetry Slams. Asheville, NC wins the team competition and Boston's Patricia Smith wins her fourth individual title.

1996. Filmmaker Paul Devlin brings a documentary crew to the Nationals in Portland to shoot *SlamNation*, which premieres at the Sundance Film Festival two years later. Providence wins with 27 teams competing. Patricia Johnson, representing Roanoke, VA, wins the individual championship.

1997. Nationals are held in Middletown, CT with 33 teams, including a team from Sweden and two Canadian teams. The Mouth Almighty team, a New York-based team named for the spoken word record label sponsoring them, wins the team competition. Cleveland's Da Boogie Man becomes the first man to win the individual title.

1998. The Nationals, held in Austin, bring 45 teams into competition, including 13 first-time teams. New York edges Dallas to win its first-ever team championship, and Chicago's Reggie Gibson wins the individual title.

1999. The 10th Annual Nationals are held in Chicago, featuring 48 teams. New York's Roger Bonair-Agard wins the individual championship. Teams from San Francisco and San Jose slam to a first-place tie. Rather than compete in a tie-breaker round, the teams decide to share the title.

2000. Nationals in Providence.

2001. Seattle hosts the Nationals.

Acknowledgments

DisClaimer by Bob Holman, reprinted from *The Collect Call of the Wild* (Henry Holt and Company, 1995), by permission of the author. *Your Father Says You Are Beautiful* by Faith Vicinanza originally appeared in *The Underwood Review*, Vol. 1 (1998). *The Emperor's Second Wife* by Adrienne Su, reprinted from *Middle Kingdom* (Alice James Books, 1997) by permission of the publisher and author. *My Father's Coat* by Marc Smith, reprinted from *Crowd Pleaser* (College Press, 1996) by permission of the author. *Chicks Up Front* by Sara Holbrook, reprinted from *Chicks Up Front* (Cleveland State University Press, 1998) by permission of the author. *In A Place Where* by Patricia A. Johnson, reprinted from *Stain My Days Blue* (Ausdoh Press, 1999) by permission of the author. *Disasterology* by Jeffrey McDaniel, reprinted from *Alibi School* (Manic D Press, 1995) by permission of the publisher and author. *Chinese Restaurant* by Justin Chin, reprinted from *Bite Hard* (Manic D Press, 1996) by permission of the publisher and author. *Grandfather's Breath* by Ray McNiece, reprinted from *The Bone-Orchard Conga* (Poetry Alive! Publications, 1997) by permission of the author. *Barefoot In The City* by Lisa Buscani, reprinted from *Jangle* (Tia Chucha Press, 1992), reprinted by permission of the author.

For more information on the National Poetry Slam, visit www.poetryslam.com

Manic D Press Books